Istiodactylus

Zhenyuanopterus

...atzegopteryx

...athus

Ludodactylus

Nemicolopterus

Brasileodactylus

Pterodaustro

Eopteranodon

...cho

Pteranodon

Domeykodactylus

Anhanguera

Pterofiltrus

Azhdarcho

...chus

Boreopterus

Dsungaripterus

Ornithocheirus

Cearadactylus

Shenzhoupterus

...erus

Feilongus

Noripterus

Haopterus

Gegepterus

Tupandactylus

...us

Nyctosaurus

Lonchognathosaurus

Uktenadactylus

Elanodactylus

Tupuxuara

...chus

Dawndraco

Phobetor

Caulkicephalus

Ningchengopterus

Quetzalcoatlus

PNSO Encyclopedia for Children

THE SECRETS OF PTEROSAURS

PNSO Encyclopedia for Children
THE SECRETS OF PTEROSAURS

Illustrations: ZHAO Chuang / Text: YANG Yang

A PNSO Production

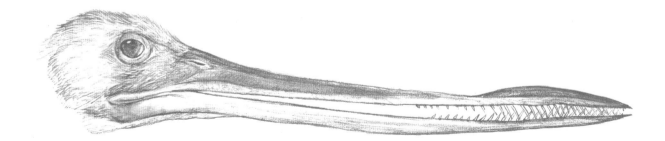

BROWN BOOKS KIDS

PNSO Encyclopedia for Children: subtitle by Yang Yang and Zhao Chuang

The Secrets of Pterosaurs

Brown Books Kids
16250 Knoll Trail Drive, Suite 205
Dallas / New York
www.BrownBooksKids.com
(972) 381-0009

A New Era in Publishing®

Publisher's Cataloging-In-Publication Data

Names: Yang, Yang (Writer of children's encyclopedia), author. | Zhao, Chuang, illustrator. | Chen, Mo, translator. | PNSO (Organization), production company.
Title: The secrets of pterosaurs / illustrations: ZHAO Chuang ; text: YANG Yang ; [translator, Chen Mo].
Description: Dallas ; New York : Brown Books Kids, [2021] | Series: PNSO encyclopedia for children ; [2] | Translated from the Chinese published in 2015. | "A PNSO production." | Interest age level: 010-012. | Include bibliographical references and index. | Summary: "Hundreds of millions of years ago, great beasts ruled on the land, beneath the surface of the water, and up above in the skies. Read about pterosaurs, the flying companions of land-dwelling dinosaurs ..."--Provided by publisher.
Identifiers: ISBN 9781612545189
Subjects: LCSH: Pterosauria--Encyclopedias, Juvenile. | CYAC: Pterosaurs--Encyclopedias.
Classification: LCC QE842 .Y36 2021 | DDC 567.903--dc23

ISBN 978-1-61254-518-9
LCCN 2021930259

Printed in China
10 9 8 7 6 5 4 3 2 1

For more information or to contact the author, please go to www.BrownBooks.com.

This book is dedicated to:

The Wright brothers (Orville Wright and Wilbur Wright).
We thank them for inventing the airplane and helping us realize the dream of flight.

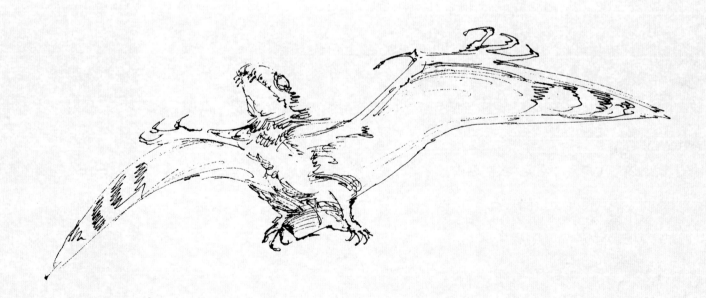

Contents List

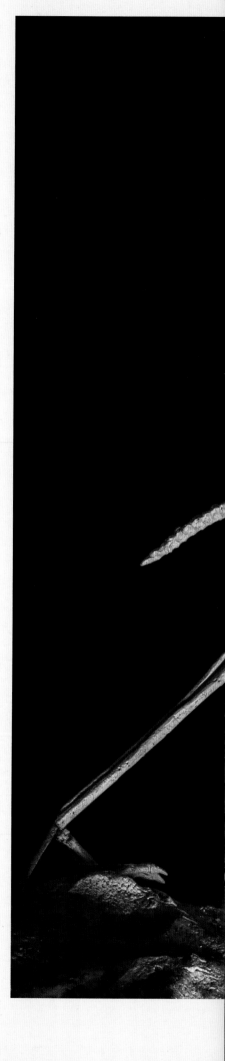

Pterosaur fossil

Table of Contents

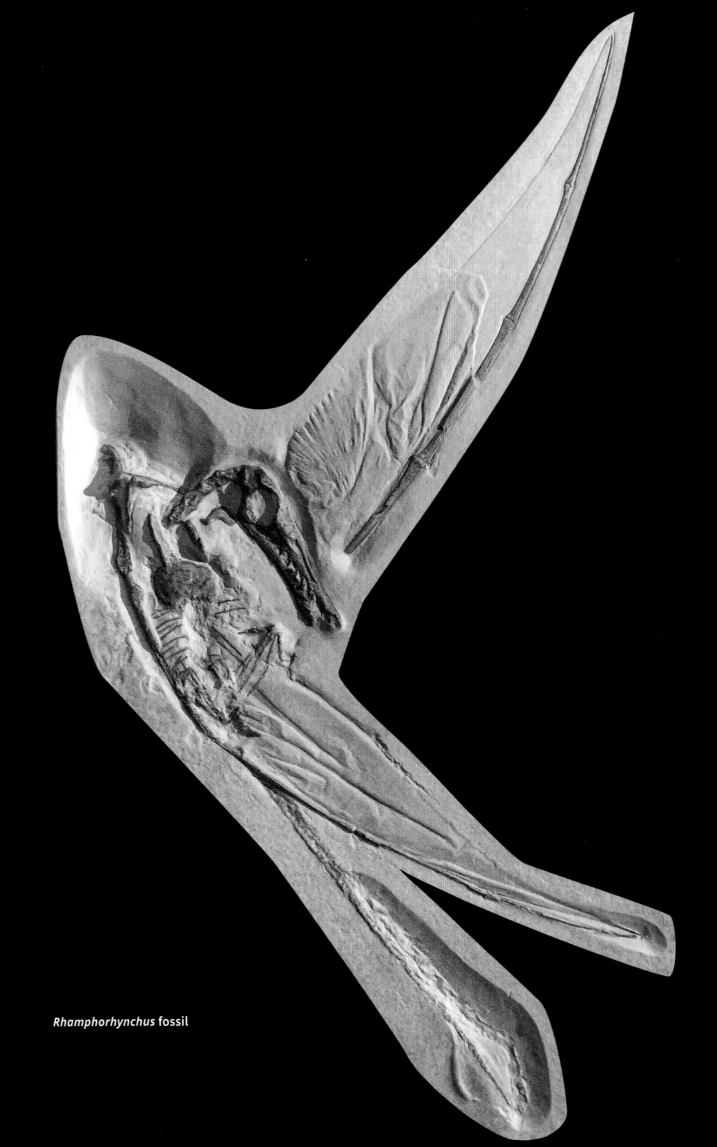

Rhamphorhynchus fossil

Table of Contents

Foreword

Paleontologist Curator and Chairman of the Division of Paleontology, AMNH Science Consultant for English Publications of PNSO Dr. Mark A. Norell's Introduction to the Works by ZHAO Chuang and YANG Yang

I am a paleontologist at one of the world's great museums. I get to spend my days surrounded by dinosaur bones. Whether it is in Mongolia excavating, in China studying, in New York analyzing data, or anywhere on the planet writing, teaching, or lecturing, dinosaurs are not only my interest, but my livelihood.

Most scientists, even the most brilliant ones, work in very closed societies. A system which, no matter how hard they try, is still unapproachable to average people. Maybe it's due to the complexities of mathematics, difficulties in understanding molecular biochemistry, or reconciling complex theory with actual data. No matter what, this behavior fosters boredom and disengagement. Personality comes in as well, and most scientists lack the communication skills necessary to make their efforts interesting and approachable. People are left being intimidated by science. But dinosaurs are special—people of all ages love them. So dinosaurs foster a great opportunity to teach science to everyone by tapping into something everyone is interested in.

That's why Yang Yang and Zhao Chuang are so important. Both are extraordinarily talented, very smart, but neither are scientists. Instead they use art and words as a medium to introduce dinosaur science to everyone from small children to grandparents—and even to scientists working in other fields!

Zhao Chuang's paintings, sculptures, drawings and films are state of the art representations of how these fantastic animals looked and behaved. They are drawn from the latest discoveries and his close collaboration with leading paleontologists. Yang Yang's writing is more than mere description. Instead she weaves stories through the narrative or makes the descriptions engaging and humorous. The subjects are so approachable that her stories can be read to small children, and young readers can discover these animals and explore science on their own. Through our fascination with dinosaurs, important concepts of geology, biology, and evolution are learned in a fun way. Zhao Chuang and Yang Yang are the world's best, and it is an honor to work with them.

Author's Preface

We are not alone in this world; we share it with others.

——A word to the fathers and mothers of our young readers

As I write this, I am sitting in the shade of my courtyard. Above in the trees, the cicadas are incessantly chirping, with their noises filling the air. Since the beginning of late spring, they have been happily chirping away every day. Happily? Well, I rarely see them; they are either hiding deep down in the dark soil biding their time until they reach maturity, or lying on the tree branches, enjoying a reclusive life. I know this without having to see them; as I listen to the sounds which tease my ear, I know that they are living a merry life in the world that we share with them.

At this moment, my daughter is chasing an ant that is moving on the ground; occasionally, she interrupts me with her giggles. She finds leaves which were blown off the trees by wind the night before and are now lying on the ground. Picking them up in bunches, she comes over to show me her new discovery. I tell her that these are leaves that have fallen from the trees. Soon after, she grabs a few rose petals, acting as if she is going to consume them. I quickly instruct her that these are flowers and that flowers cannot be eaten. Maybe she does not understand what I am saying; she has just learned to crawl, and she is still unable to talk. Because of this she probably does not recognize and identify the ants, leaves, and flowers, but nevertheless, she gets great enjoyment from watching them, just as she does from seeing me, as she giggles playfully. For her, there are very few differences between the ants, leaves, and flowers on the one hand, and her mom and dad, aunts and uncles on the other. She has great curiosity toward all these things which share this world with her.

I can't really identify at what point adults gradually begin to lose this magical sense of curiosity, or when we begin to overlook all of the other types of life and arrogantly consider humans as the most important subjects, simply because now we are the predominant group on this planet.

The irony is that if there is no other life, humans would no longer be able to support themselves and would perish. However, we often do not think in this way. We are accustomed to understanding life through such a paradigm: chicken is delicious food, from which you can make roast chicken or smoked chicken; the beef we get from cattle tastes good and has high nutritional value. We are often indoctrinated with such knowledge, so it is no surprise that this often inadvertently breeds our selfish arrogance.

I often find myself thinking about this problem, so for the longest time, I have desired to write an encyclopedia for children, one that introduces them to a wide variety of other types of life. This encyclopedic book should not be like ones written for adults; it is not merely a large number of details showing an animal's length, height, and weight. Its purpose is to be far more than a pile of data, to go beyond just a list of knowledge and facts; the essence of this work is meant to be like the chorus of afternoon cicadas. You cannot see them, yet you hear their voices, just like those ants which my daughter find enchanting—you forge a close connection with them despite not knowing their specifics. For children, everything in this world is incredibly fresh. They want to know: beyond themselves, their family, their kindergarten teachers, and fellow students, what else is out there in this world? In addition to their home, their kindergarten, and the city that they live in, how much further beyond does this world extend to? They want to move beyond the present and the past that they can remember to know how far the world will go. Their curiosity is a key which unlocks the entire world. All they ask us is to leave the door open. They can figure out the rest on their own.

Hence, our collection of stories within the PNSO Encyclopedia for Children is meant to impress our children with an understanding of the world beyond humans. Children should realize that this world is not only for us; others share it with us. The "others" may be other forms of life or something wonderful that exists in our human imagination. In short, these exist in our present world, whether in our day-to-day reality or the magical expanses of our imagination.

To be aware of their existence is more than a form of knowledge. It is a strength by which our inner world expands and broadens. If that happens, we will be less likely to become arrogant because of our ignorance, to begrudge over small things, or to hinder our long-term future because of immediate gains. We can avoid being selfish, narrow-minded, and fearful. We should respect all lives because they have accompanied us throughout our existence and are sharing this world with us. The world is so dauntingly big; it is vital that we work together in harmony with each other to move forward.

Often, the babbling of a young child constantly reminds me how important it is to keep alive the curiosity of childhood. It is that curiosity that allows us to walk humbly in this vast world. I hope that as you read this book with your children, you may nurture their sense of curiosity and accompany them in exploring this wondrous world.

杨杨

YANG Yang

August 1, 2015, in Beijing

IVPP V16866

Jianchangnathus robustus fossil

Notes for Reading

1 **Period of Existence of Pterosaurs**
(For single pterosaur images with no background)

2 **Scales:** 50 cm, 1 m, 5 m, 25 m
Reference objects: basketball, father, mother, boy, girl, bus, plane
Showing pterosaurs' sizes: pterosaur's silhouette (when the size of the pterosaur
is less than 1 unit of the scale), pterosaur's outline

Millions of Years Ago	252.17 ±0.06	~247.2	~237		201.3 ±0.2		174.1 ±1.0	163.5 ±1.0
Epoch	Early Triassic	Middle Triassic	Late Triassic		Early Jurassic		Middle Jurassic	
Period			Triassic			Jurassic		
Era								
Eon								

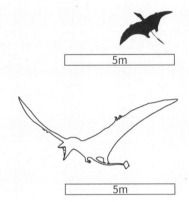

5m

5m

CMYK color codes for scales, reference objects, and diagrams showing pterosaurs' sizes

Dark background: C0 M0 Y0 K80

Light background: C0 M0 Y0 K20

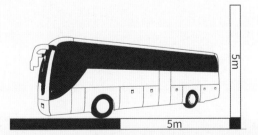

5m

5m

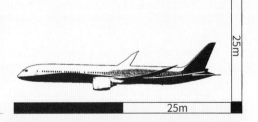

25m

25m

~145.0

100.5

66.0

Late Jurassic

Early Cretaceous

Late Cretaceous

Cretaceous

Mesozoic

Phanerozoic Eon

Sky-Conquering Pterosaurs

The infinite sky is mysterious. When we lie on a lawn and look at the sky, some of us hope to have a pair of wings and fly into it to take a closer look.

The vast sky is home to countless animals. From the earliest insects to beautiful birds, these animals spread their wings and fly to explore endless possibilities and greater freedom.

The sky is mysterious in the sense that countless lives were born to fly in the sky for hundreds of millions of years and then disappeared. The traces of their flight had long been blown away, leaving only the stories that they had created.

Well, if we can build a castle using those stories and live inside it, it will be as if we are flying. In this castle, we can talk to those flyers about the sky.

This is a great dream. Have you expected that dream to come true? The gate to that castle of stories sits right in front of us. Turn the page, and we will enter the castle and see its most mysterious inhabitant, the pterosaurs.

Why are pterosaurs mysterious?

Because they are special. They were the first vertebrates that flew.

They were the most successful flyers of all time. A little wind would send them soaring in the sky, traveling thousands of kilometers.

They were perfect aviators with huge wingspans that collectively covered almost the entire sky.

Although they have disappeared, we are still able to visit the world in which they once lived, because we are now in the castle of stories.

Pterosaurs in the Castle

Pterosaurs were the loyal companions of dinosaurs. While the giant dinosaurs roamed Earth, the pterosaurs were the undisputed rulers in the sky.

They created countless glories. But 66 million years ago, like non-avian dinosaurs, they eventually failed to live through the terrible mass extinction, leaving the sky to be occupied by the fledgling birds. The disappeared pterosaurs left us great stories and precious fossils, the latter hidden in rocks.

In 1964, a team of paleontologists discovered a pterosaur skull and a few other parts in the Junggar Basin, Xinjiang. They carefully dug it out and named it *Dsungaripterus*.

They speculated that this *Dsungaripterus*, once roaming the Mesozoic sky, had been killed by a violent storm hundreds of millions of years ago. It fell into a lake and was gradually covered by sediment at the bottom of the lake. As time went on, the soft flesh of its body rotted, while its hard bones were covered by sand, petrified, and eventually fossilized.

Tens of millions of years later, the once crystal clear lake has become a dry desert. Many years of wind and sunshine gradually weathered the rocks, revealing the fossil.

Among all pterosaurs, *Dsungaripterus* was lucky. After the pterosaurs' deaths, their thin bones could be either devoured by scavengers or decomposed by microorganisms, so very few pterosaur fossils could be so well-preserved. At present, we have only about 120 pterosaur genera identified. What we know about them is just the tip of the iceberg of these great animals, and more fossils remain to be discovered.

As we roam around the castle, we will see beautiful pterosaurs reconstructed from these fossils.

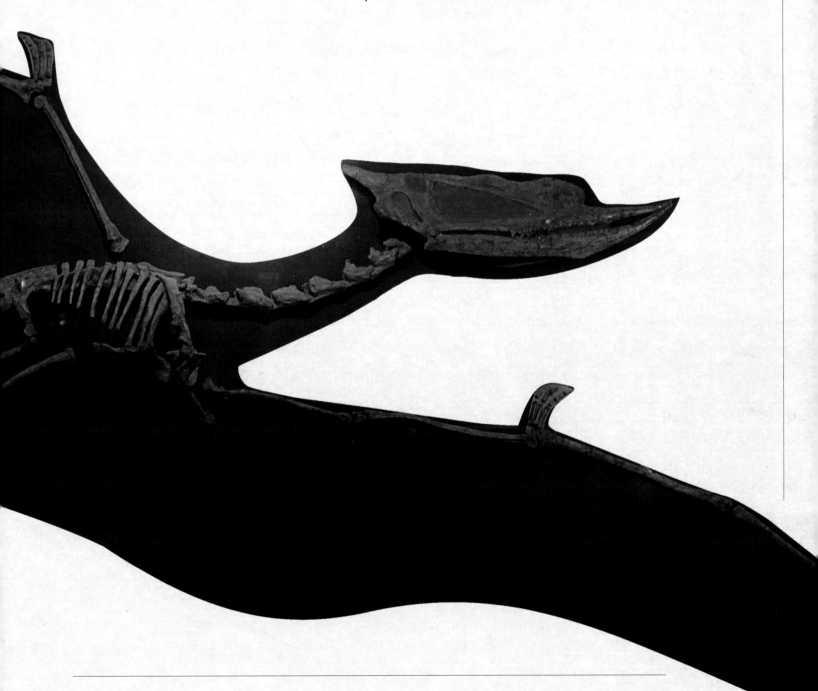

Origin of Pterosaurs

Who were the ancestors of pterosaurs? What were they like before they could fly? How did they fly? In adapting to flight, pterosaurs' bones must have changed a lot from their ancestors. Despite having found many pterosaur fossils, we still can't answer these questions accurately. It looks as if pterosaurs appeared out of nowhere and took over the sky overnight.

Still, scientists were trying to figure out the pterosaurs' origins. After extensive research, they believe that the pterosaurs' ancestors were probably related to *Scleromochlus*, *Lagosuchus*, and *Herrerasaurus*.

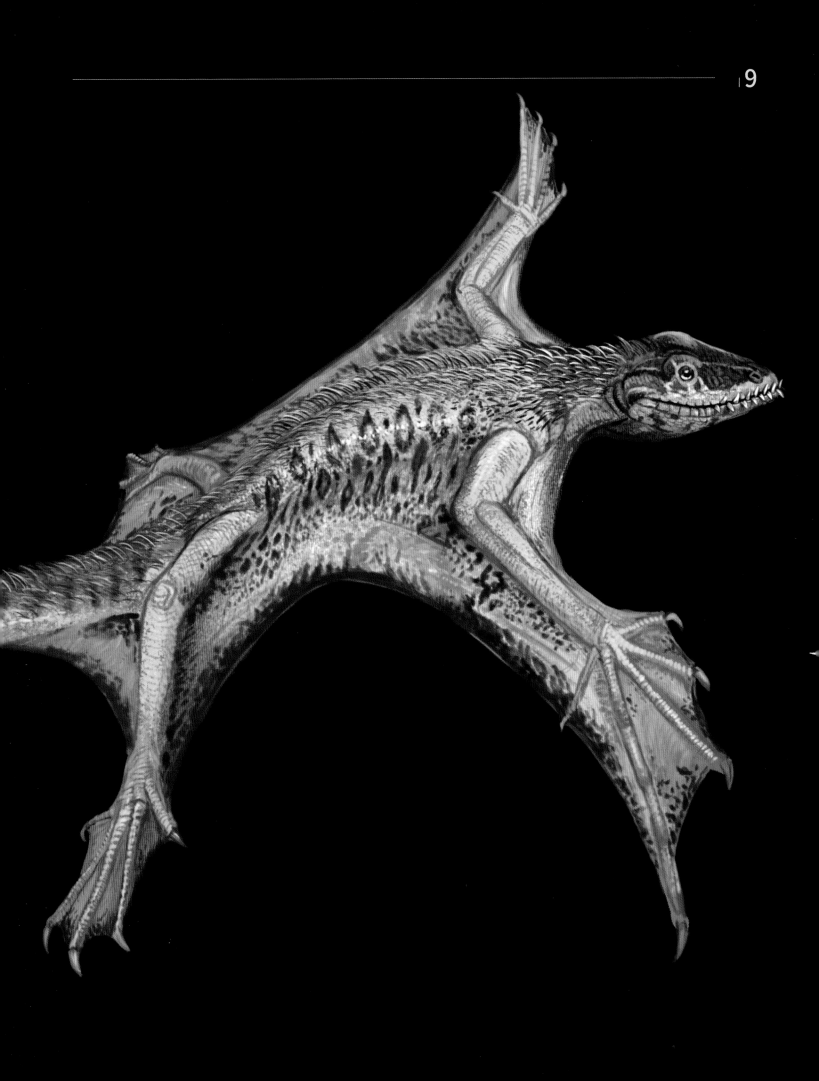

Origins of Nonpterodactyloid Fossils

Compiled by: PNSO

26 | *Sordes*
Fossil Origin: Kazakhstan, Asia

28 | *Pterorhynchus*
Fossil Origin: China, Asia

30 | *Sericipterus*
Fossil Origin: China, Asia

32 | *Fenghuangopterus*
Fossil Origin: China, Asia

50 | *Batrachognathus*
Fossil Origin: Kazakhstan, Asia

54 | *Jeholopterus*
Fossil Origin: China, Asia

56 | *Dendrorhynchoides*
Fossil Origin: China, Asia

58 | *Kunpengopterus*
Fossil Origin: China, Asia

60 | *Darwinopterus*
Fossil Origin: China, Asia

62 | *Wukongopterus*
Fossil Origin: China, Asia

64 | *Angustinaripterus*
Fossil Origin: China, Asia

18 | *Cacibupteryx*
Fossil Origin: Cuba, North America

20 | *Nesodactylus*
Fossil Origin: Cuba, North America

24 | *Harpactognathus*
Fossil Origin: United States, North America

 Asia   South America   Africa   Europe   North America   Oceania

Sinopterus dongi fossil

Period of Existence of Nonpterodactyloid in the Mesozoic Era

Compiled by: PNSO

34	*Carniadactylus*	Triassic Period
38	*Caviramus*	Triassic Period
40	*Austriadactylus*	Triassic Period
42	*Eudimorphodon*	Triassic Period
44	*Raeticodactylus*	Triassic Period
46	*Peteinosaurus*	Triassic Period

Fenghuangopterus fossil

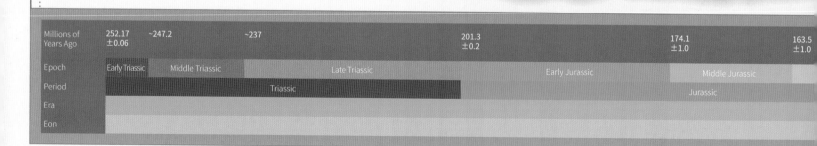

Millions of Years Ago	252.17 ±0.06	~247.2	~237		201.3 ±0.2		174.1 ±1.0	163.5 ±1.0
Epoch	Early Triassic	Middle Triassic	Late Triassic			Early Jurassic	Middle Jurassic	
Period		Triassic					Jurassic	
Era								
Eon								

~145.0   100.5   66.0

Late Jurassic   Early Cretaceous   Late Cretaceous

Cretaceous

Mesozoic

Phanerozoic Eon

Rhamphocephalus

Terrifying fish killer

With a wingspan of only two meters, the medium-size *Rhamphocephalus* still found hunting easy, thanks to its extremely sharp teeth. Any fish that jumped out of the water would quickly dive back in, running for their lives if they caught a glimpse of its shadow!

    Rhamphocephalus had a narrow head, a thin body, and a long tail.

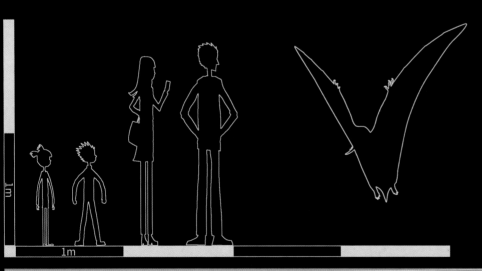

1m

Millions of Years Ago	252.17 ±0.06	~247.2	~237		201.3 ±0.2		174.1 ±1.0		163.5 ±1.0
Epoch	Early Triassic	Middle Triassic		Late Triassic		Early Jurassic		Middle Jurassic	
Period			Triassic				Jurassic		
Era									
Eon									

Rhamphocephalus

Body size: Wingspan of about 2 meters
Diet: Fish
Period of existence: Jurassic
Fossil origin: United Kingdom, Europe

100.5

66.0

Late Jurassic

Early Cretaceous

Late Cretaceous

Cretaceous

Me

Phanerozoic Eon

Dorygnathus
with its spear-like mouth

What is a spear? It is a weapon that the ancient people used in fighting. Look at this pterosaur. Surprisingly, it had a spear-like mouth, with many spikes growing on the "spear."

It is called a *Dorygnathus*, and those terrifying spikes were the teeth that extended out from the front part of its mouth. They were great fishing tools. *Dorygnathus* also had straight, less scary-looking smaller teeth in the rear of its mouth. It was common that primitive pterosaurs had more than one type of teeth.

Dorygnathus

Body size: Wingspan of about 1.5–3 meters
Diet: Fish
Period of existence: Jurassic
Fossil origin: Germany and France, Europe

1m

1m

Cacibupteryx

Late Jurassic "pirate of the Caribbean"

Cacibupteryx lived in the Caribbean region in Late Jurassic, when the Caribbean Sea first appeared, linking Western Tethys Ocean and the eastern Pacific Ocean, and attracted marine animals from both oceans. The larger *Cacibupteryx* enriched its diet by eating these animals, and it was indeed the "pirate of the Caribbean" then! Often flying low over the sea, it used its long tail and the bony vane on it to steer. As soon as it saw prey, it would strike quickly and accurately.

50cm

50cm

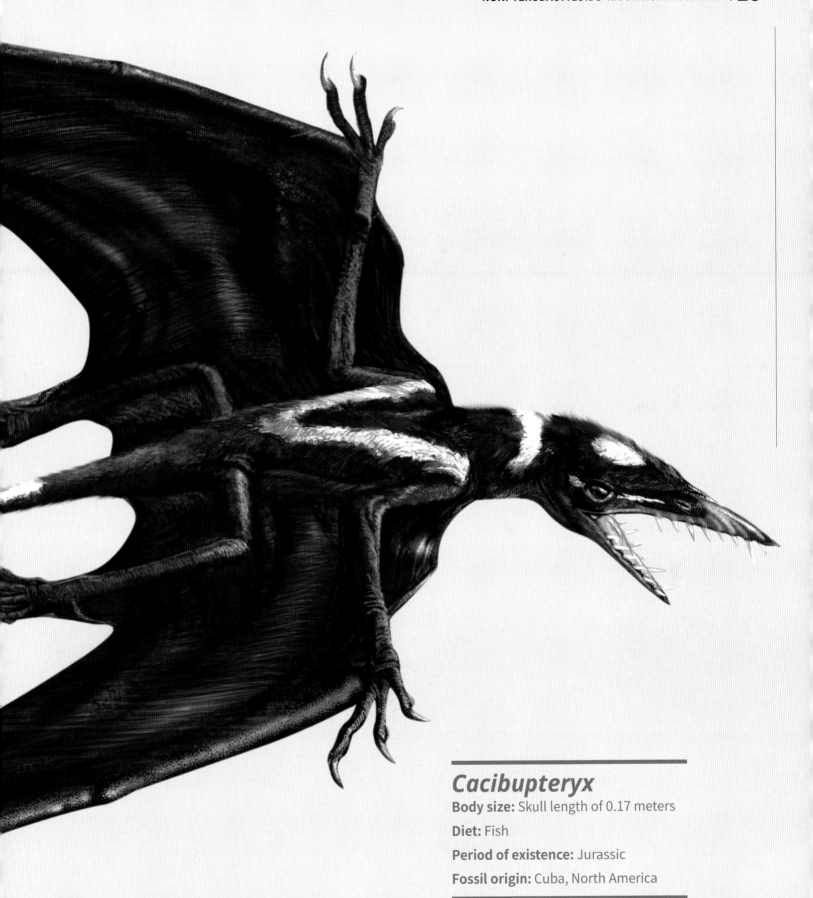

Cacibupteryx

Body size: Skull length of 0.17 meters

Diet: Fish

Period of existence: Jurassic

Fossil origin: Cuba, North America

Hard-working
Nesodactylus

The sun had just risen, and the forest was still shrouded in a gray mist. Ferns that covered the ground were about to shake off the dews and wake up from their sleep. But the *Nesodactylus* had already prepared its breakfast.

Those sleepy pterosaurs were probably drooling enviously. They always thought that the *Nesodactylus* was lucky. What they did not know was that the *Nesodactylus* was the most industrious in the forest because it always got up earlier and slept later than everyone else.

Nesodactylus

Body size: Wingspan of 2 meters
Diet: Fish
Period of existence: Jurassic
Fossil origin: Cuba, North America

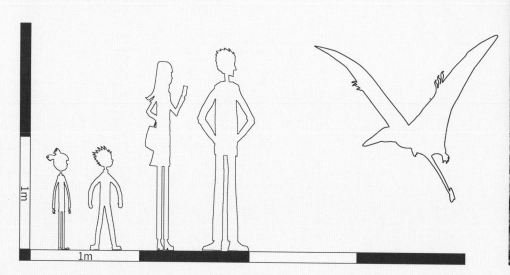

Scaphognathus
What was it doing?

Dark clouds covered the sky, and the gigantic *Bothrio-spondylus* walked quickly, hoping to get home before the rain got its skin wet.

As it was walking, a *Scaphognathus* hurried out of its cave and headed for the lake.

The *Bothriospondylus* looked curiously at the strange-looking pterosaur, not knowing that this *Scaphognathus* was taking the opportunity to catch fish. Before the heavy rain, the fish in the lake will come close to the surface, making themselves easy catches.

Scaphognathus

Body size: Wingspan of 1 meter
Diet: Fish
Period of existence: Jurassic
Fossil origin: Germany, Europe

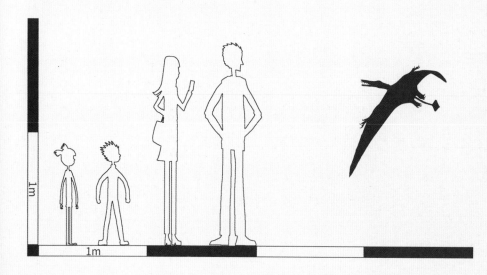

Harpactognathus

Largest hegemon of the Late Jurassic sky

With a body length of three meters, formidably sharp teeth, and a pair of eyes that target every prey, the *Harpactognathus* was the greatest hegemon in the Late Jurassic period.

It liked to live by lakes, but its food was not limited to the easy-to-catch fish. Though catching the small animals on land would be more of a challenge, those were its preferred targets.

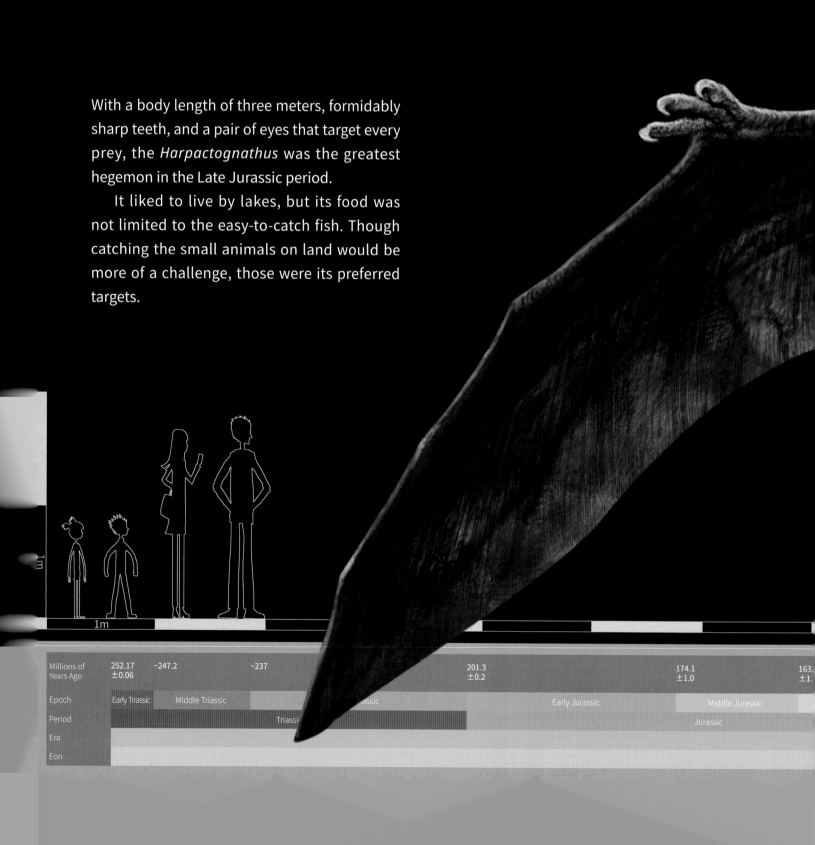

1m

Millions of Years Ago	252.17 ±0.06	~247.2		~237			201.3 ±0.2		174.1 ±1.0	163. ±1.
Epoch	Early Triassic	Middle Triassic			...assic			Early Jurassic	Middle Jurassic	
Period				Triassi					Jurassic	
Era										
Eon										

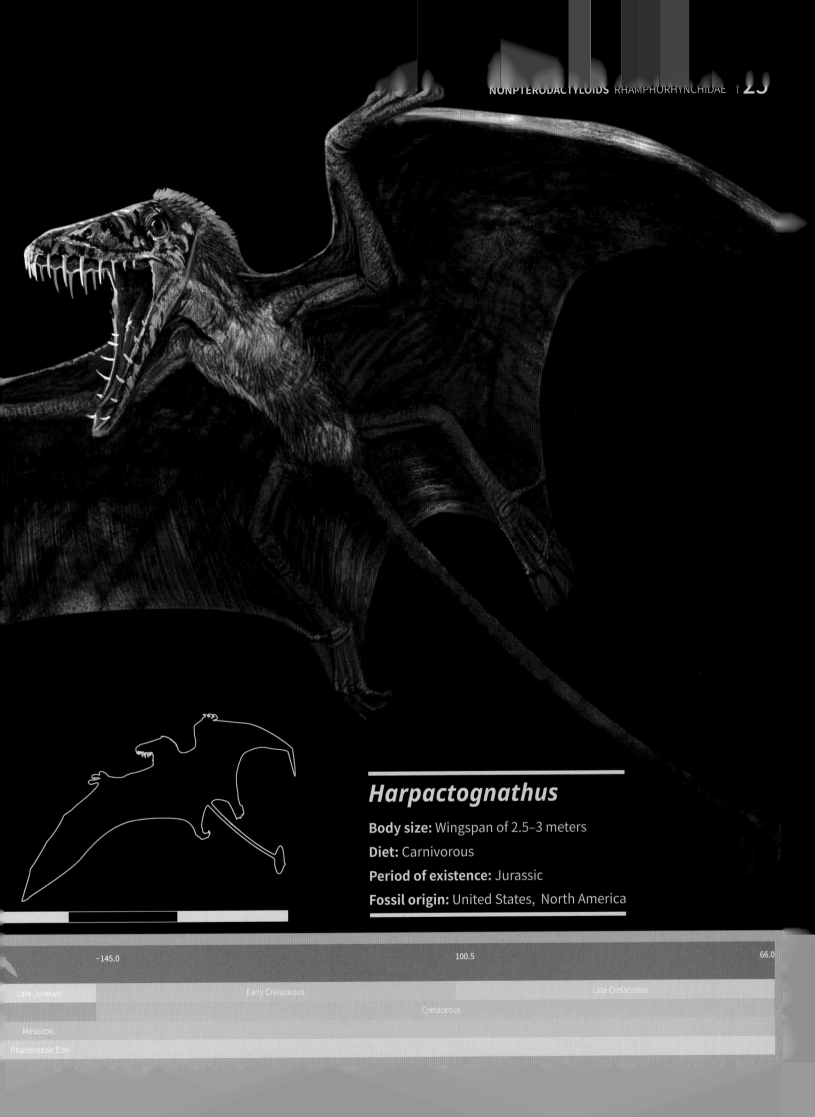

Harpactognathus

Body size: Wingspan of 2.5–3 meters

Diet: Carnivorous

Period of existence: Jurassic

Fossil origin: United States, North America

~145.0 100.5 66.0

Late Jurassic Early Cretaceous Late Cretaceous

Cretaceous

Mesozoic

Phanerozoic Eon

Sordes
Not evil-looking

The name of *Sordes* means evil spirits in the local language, but it does not look devilish at all.

It had neither sharp, extended, nor terrifying teeth, and its wingspan was not particularly large. On the contrary, the feathers fully covering its body made it look fluffy and cute!

50cm

50cm

Millions of Years Ago	252.17 ±0.06	~247.		201.3 ±0.2		174.1 ±1.0		163.5 ±1.0
Epoch	Early Triassic		Late Triassic		Early Jurassic		Middle Jurassic	
Period						Jurassic		
Era								
Eon								

Sordes

Body size: Wingspan of about 0.63 meters
Diet: Fish
Period of existence: Jurassic
Fossil origin: Kazakhstan, Asia

~145.0   100.5   66.0

Late Jurassic   Early Cretaceous   Late Cretaceous

                                    Cretaceous

Mesozoic

Phanerozoic Eon

Gluttonous
Pterorhynchus

The storm was arriving, with strong wind carrying waves high in the air.

A *Pterorhynchus* flew through the waves, trying to get back into its nest before the heavy downpour. Its tail, as long as its wingspan, fluttered in the air, cutting through the waves that kept rising towards it.

Suddenly, a dragonfly, which was also rushing home, was caught by the wind and brought towards it. Excitedly, the *Pterorhynchus* opened its mouth. Getting away from the rain was important, but this was a good snack in the storm, one not to be missed!

Pterorhynchus

Body size: Length about 0.85 meters

Diet: Carnivorous

Period of existence: Jurassic

Fossil origin: China, Asia

Sericipterus
that fed on small animals

Most of the pterosaur fossils discovered by scientists are buried in marine or lacustrine sediments, suggesting that these pterosaurs lived by seas or lakes and fed on fish. *Sericipterus* was different. Its fossil was buried in terrestrial sediment. Scientists speculate that it probably lived far away from water, so it might not eat a lot of fish. Instead, its main diet was small land animals.

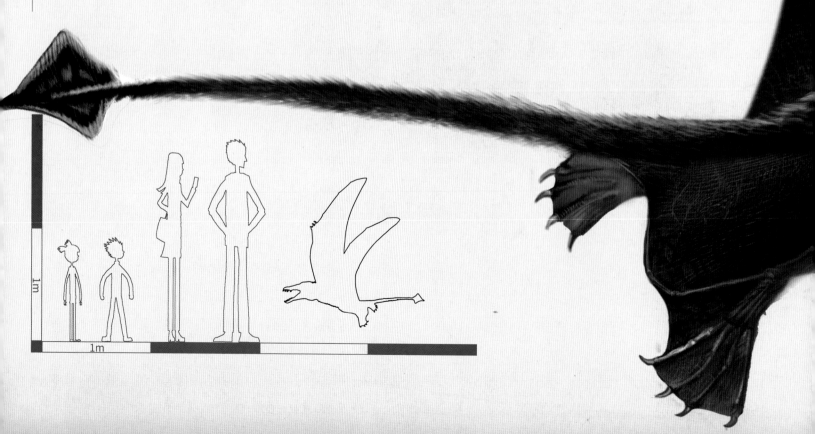

1m

1m

Sericipterus

Body size: Wingspan of about 1.73 meters
Diet: Carnivorous
Period of existence: Jurassic
Fossil origin: China, Asia

Fenghuangopterus

Body size: Wingspan of about 1.5 meters

Diet: Carnivorous

Period of existence: Jurassic

Fossil origin: China, Asia

1m

1m

Millions of Years Ago	252.17 ±0.06	~247.2	~237		01.3 ±0.2		174.1 ±1.0	163. ±1.0
Epoch	Early Triassic	Middle Triassic				Early Jurassic		Middle Jurassic
Period			Triassic				Jurassic	
Era								
Eon								

Fenghuangopterus
Does not look like a phoenix at all

With a name that means "phoenix," *Fenghuangopterus* did not look like a phoenix and was probably less graceful. It liked to open its big mouth, showing its sharp and terrifying teeth.

In fact, scientists named it because its fossils were found in Fenghuang Mountain in Liaoning Province, China.

The *Fenghuangopterus*'s body was strong, and its thick neck was almost as long as its head. It had no beautiful crest on its head.

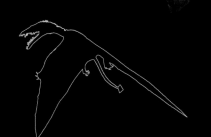

~145.0   100.5   66.0

Late Jurassic   Early Cretaceous   Late Cretaceous

Cretaceous

Mesozoic

Phanerozoic Eon

Carniadactylus

Body size: Wingspan of 1 meter
Diet: Insects
Period of existence: Triassic
Fossil origin: Italy, Europe

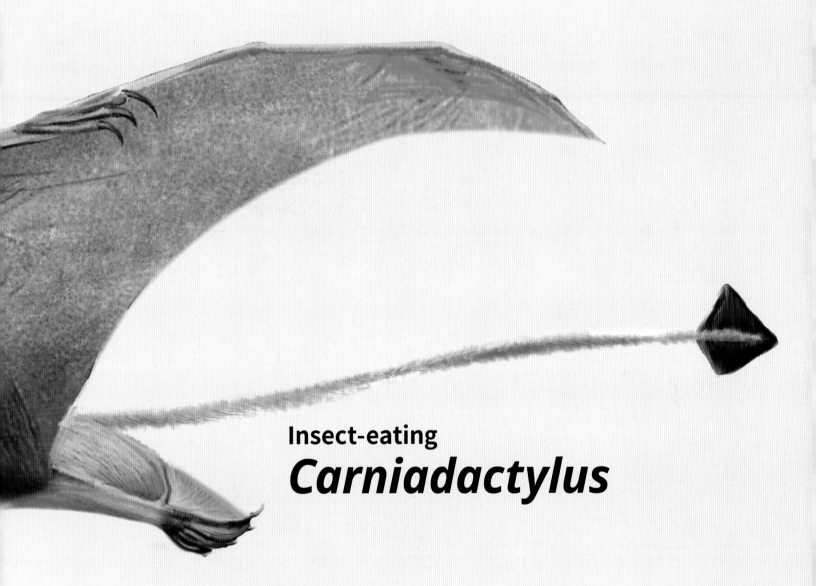

Insect-eating
Carniadactylus

Many pterosaurs enjoyed eating fish, but the *Carniadactylus* probably thought removing the hard fish scales was too troublesome, so it preferred eating softer insects.

Of course, it was not a wild guess. The fossils of the *Carniadactylus* showed no significant wear on their teeth, suggesting that they preferred to eat foods that did not need to be processed.

Night-hunting
Campylognathoides

Campylognathoides had a pair of big eyes. Therefore scientists thought it had excellent vision, enabling it to see clearly at night. So, it might go out hunting at night. While night hunting was bad for its sleep, doing so would be a good tradeoff because it would face fewer competitors for food.

Ever since scientists discovered pterosaurs, they have been wondering whether pterosaurs could walk on the ground. They got the answer from *Campylognathoides*. Its fossil tells us that many pterosaurs walked clumsily on the ground, like a human child who had not yet learned to walk.

Campylognathoides

Body size: Wingspan of 1–1.825 meters
Diet: Fish
Period of existence: Jurassic
Fossil origin: Germany, Europe

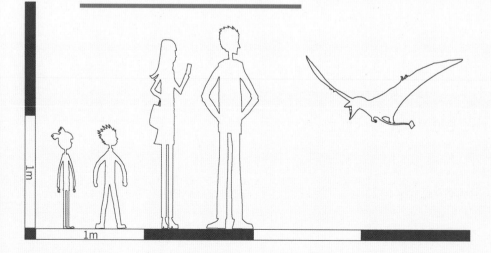

Caviramus

Flying above present-day Switzerland

The *Caviramus* was one of the precious few pterosaurs found in Switzerland. Scientists had to guess its looks from its relatives, making the same guesses as when they reconstructed the *Angustinaripterus*.

Scientists speculate that the *Caviramus* had a long and pointed head, large eyes, and sharp teeth. In addition, it had long wings and a thin body. Its tail had a bony vane that could steer in flight.

Caviramus

Body size: Unknown

Diet: Fish

Period of existence: Triassic

Fossil origin: Switzerland, Europe

An *Austriadactylus*
rushing towards its love

It was once again the mating season. Flapping its wings, the *Austriadactylus* flew over the jungle.

It moved its light body gracefully and rapidly, with a diamond-shaped bony vane on its tail steering. Its heart was pumping because it was going to meet its lover!

Look at its gorgeous crest, as colorful as the setting sun, would surely get the lover's attention!

Austriadactylus

Body size: Wingspan of about 1.2 meters

Diet: Carnivorous

Period of existence: Triassic

Fossil origin: Austria, Europe

Eudimorphodon

A rock climber

Eudimorphodon was both an excellent flyer and a master rock climber. It often nimbly climbed the rocks on the shore and ambushed its prey from there. Then a hunt began.

A flying *Eudimorphodon* slowly landed, using its digits to grip a rock tightly, while its big eyes were staring at the sea's rolling waves.

Suddenly, its eyes were fixed on something in the foam. It was not merely looking at the sea. What it really liked was the fish that took a ride on the waves to see what was above sea.

It held its breath and tightened every muscle, and struck when the wave fell from the highest point. It firmly held the fish in its mouth, flew back, and made a soft landing. Now it was time to enjoy its meal.

Eudimorphodon

Body size: Wingspan of 1 meter

Diet: Fish

Period of existence: Triassic

Fossil origin: Italy, Europe

Millions of Years Ago	252.17 ±0.06	~247.2	~237		201.3 ±0.2		174.1 ±1.0	163. ±1.0
Epoch	Early Triassic	Middle Triassic	Late Triassic			Early Jurassic		Middle Jurassic
Period			Triassic				Jurassic	
Era								
Eon								

~145.0

66.0

Late Jurassic

Early Cretaceous

Late Cretaceous

Mesozoic

Phanerozoic Eon

Predating
Raeticodactylus

A *Raeticodactylus*, with its big mouth wide open and sharp teeth extended, scurried across the sky. It paid no attention to the gorgeous colors. It flapped its broad wings as if trying to fan away the clouds that stood in its way.

Where was it going? Look at that group of frolicking fish on the sea not far away. The *Raeticodactylus* could be drooling at this moment!

Raeticodactylus

Body size: Wingspan of about 1.35 meters

Diet: Carnivorous

Period of existence: Triassic

Fossil origin: Switzerland, Europe

1m

1m

Peteinosaurus
At the side of dinosaurs

Pterosaurs were dinosaurs' best friends. They emerged at almost the same time and disappeared together.

When the skinny *Coelophysis* was not yet a hegemon as later dinosaurs were, it struggled to survive under the shadow of bigger guys. The flying *Peteinosaurus* had much good time with it. Although the *Peteinosaurus* did not catch prey for it or defeat its enemies, the companionship nevertheless made *Coelophysis* less afraid!

Peteinosaurus

Body size: Length about 0.6 meters

Diet: Insects

Period of existence: Triassic

Fossil origin: Italy, Europe

Dimorphodon

with two types of teeth

Dimorphodon had a small body and a big head. People often question if it could fly nimbly with such a large head. Well, we should not have worried about that. Its skull had three large holes to reduce weight.

Apart from its big head, its distinctive feature was its teeth. Like some primitive pterosaurs, it had two types of teeth—the long ones in the front of the jaw and the small, pointed ones in the back.

Dimorphodon

Body size: Wingspan of 1.45 meters

Diet: Carnivorous

Period of existence: Jurassic

Fossil origin: United Kingdom, Europe

1m

1m

Frog-like
Batrachognathus

Batrachognathus looked like a flying frog. Its lower jaw looked like a frog, and its skull fossil was also in the shape of one.

Paleontologists think that as they flew, they would open their mouths to catch insects. Unfortunately, they lacked a frog-like sticky tongue that could extend out and catch insects, otherwise hunting would be easier.

Unlike most nonpterodactyloids, which had long tails, Batrachognathus had a short, almost negligible tail.

Batrachognathus

Body size: Wingspan of about 0.5 meters
Diet: Insects
Period of existence: Jurassic
Fossil origin: Kazakhstan, Asia

50cm

50cm

The happy life of
Anurognathus
and sauropods

The rainy season nourished the plants such that they grew wildly, and fresh leaves appeared on all of the trees overnight.

A huge sauropod was grazing the leaves like a lawnmower. Quickly, the branches became bare. Having enough food gave it a very good mood.

Suddenly, a few blood-sucking insects flew over its head and started buzzing. It was annoyed. The pesky noise was terribly unpleasant. It swung its long tail powerfully, but it had no effect, and the little pests became more excited by its resistance.

Anurognathus swooped down quickly and gracefully, landed about half a meter from its eyes, and accurately swallowed one insect, which was about to draw blood.

The feasting insects were scared and fled. The sauropod could finally have its meal in peace, while the rejoicing *Anurognathus* was happily chewing the food that the sauropod had attracted!

50cm

50cm

Anurognathus

Body size: Wingspan of about 0.5 meters

Diet: Insects

Period of existence: Jurassic

Fossil origin: Germany, Europe

"Fluffy"
Jeholopterus

One adjective to describe *Jeholopterus* is "fluffy." Scientists studying *Jeholopterus* fossils found that its entire body was covered with short and coarse hairs. These hairs could regulate *Jeholopterus*'s body temperature, make it a better flyer, and act as a muffler when it hunted.

Jeholopterus

Body size: Wingspan of about 0.9 meters

Diet: Carnivorous

Period of existence: Jurassic

Fossil origin: China, Asia

Panicking
Dendrorhynchoides

A *Tianyulong*, fully covered in spikes, was looking for a cave to spend the night in. It did not expect to run into a group of resting *Dendrorhynchoides*.

The *Dendrorhynchoides*, frightened by the arrival of this ugly and unexpected guest, screamed and scattered.

The unsuspecting *Dendrorhynchoides* stared at those fleeing *Dendrorhynchoides* and had no idea what happened. It simply wanted to stay over for a night. Why was everyone so scared?

Dendrorhynchoides

Body size: Wingspan of about 0.4 meters
Diet: Insects
Period of existence: Cretaceous
Fossil origin: China, Asia

Kunpengopterus
which had its hair preserved

Although many pterosaurs had feathers, most of these were speculation. Few pterosaur fossils were found to contain feathers. *Kunpengopterus* was lucky in the sense that scientists found impressions of feathers on their fossils.

The fossil showed that the top of its skull had feather impressions, suggesting that at least the top of its head had beautiful hair, like what we see in the image here.

Kunpengopterus

Body size: Wingspan of about 0.7 meters
Diet: Fish
Period of existence: Jurassic
Fossil origin: China, Asia

Darwinopterus
A caring family

As soon as the day turned bright, *Darwinopterus* got up and went hunting. But the little animals seemed to know it was coming and had hidden in advance. It had flown a long distance, but the only thing it caught was a lean lizard. Despite being hungry, it did not swallow the lizard but brought the food home to its wife, who was hatching eggs.

Darwinopterus

Body size: Wingspan of 1 meter
Diet: Carnivorous
Period of existence: Jurassic
Fossil origin: China, Asia

1m

1m

Wukongopterus

Less powerful than the monkey king

Despite having the same name as Sun Wukong, the monkey king, the *Wukongopterus* knew no powerful tricks. However, it was probably a better flyer than the monkey king!

Look, it was taking off from a tree and about to chase the fish playing near the water surface. Its beautiful wings roared through the air, casting a long shadow in the water.

Wukongopterus

Body size: Wingspan of about 0.73 meters

Diet: Fish

Period of existence: Jurassic

Fossil origin: China, Asia

Angustinaripterus

with very few fossils

With slim bones, pterosaur fossils were usually more difficult to preserve than dinosaur ones. *Angustinaripterus*, for example, had only one partial skull fossil.

With so little fossil evidence, how did scientists reconstruct its model?

If there was little fossil evidence, scientists have to turn to the appearance of the relatives. Their analysis showed that the *Angustinaripterus* was of medium height. It had a short, powerful neck, stout forelegs, and a long tail with a bony vane.

Angustinaripterus

Body size: Wingspan of about 2 meters

Diet: Fish

Period of existence: Jurassic

Fossil origin: China, Asia

Origins of Pterodactyloid Fossils

Compiled by: PNSO

70 | *Archaeoistiodactylus*
Fossil Origin: China, Asia

72 | *Longchengpterus*
Fossil Origin: China, Asia

74 | *Nurhachius*
Fossil Origin: China, Asia

80 | *Istiodactylus*
Fossil Origin: Asia and Europe

86 | *Haopterus*
Fossil Origin: China, Asia

96 | *Boreopterus*
Fossil Origin: China, Asia

98 | *Feilongus*
Fossil Origin: China, Asia

104 | *Zhenyuanopterus*
Fossil Origin: China, Asia

112 | *Pterofiltrus*
Fossil Origin: China, Asia

118 | *Gegepterus*
Fossil Origin: China, Asia

120 | *Elanodactylus*
Fossil Origin: China, Asia

122 | *Ningchengopterus*
Fossil Origin: China, Asia

128 | *Nemicolopterus*
Fossil Origin: China, Asia

138 | *Dsungaripterus*
Fossil Origin: Asia and Africa

142 | *Noripterus*
Fossil Origin: China, Asia

144 | *Lonchognathosaurus*
Fossil Origin: China, Asia

146 | *Phobetor*
Fossil Origin: China, Asia

150 | *Eopteranodon*
Fossil Origin: China, Asia

152 | *Azhdarcho*
Fossil Origin: Uzbekistan, Asia

154 | *Shenzhoupterus*
Fossil Origin: China, Asia

160 | *Aralazhdarcho*
Fossil Origin: Central Asia

84 | *Ornithocheirus*
Fossil Origin: Europe and South America

90 | *Caulkicephalus*
Fossil Origin: United Kingdom, Europe

106 | *Ctenochasma*
Fossil Origin: Germany and France, Europe

114 | *Plataleorhynchus*
Fossil Origin: United Kingdom, Europe

124 | *Pterodactylus*
Fossil Origin: Germany, Europe

134 | *Altmuehlopterus*
Fossil Origin: Germany, Europe

136 | *Germanodactylus*
Fossil Origin: Germany, Europe

140 | *Normannognathus*
Fossil Origin: France, Europe

148 | *Hatzegopteryx*
Fossil Origin: Romania, Europe

 Asia   **South America**   **Africa**   **Europe**   **North America**   **Oceania**

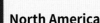

Period of Existence of Pterodactyloids in the Mesozoic Era

Compiled by: PNSO

70 | **Archaeoistiodactylus**
Jurassic Period

106 | **Ctenochasma**
Jurassic Period

124 | **Pterodactylus**
Jurassic Period

126 | **Tendaguripterus**
Jurassic Period

132 | **Herbstosaurus**
Jurassic Period

134 | **Altmuehlopterus**
Jurassic Period

136 | **Germanodactylus**
Jurassic Period

140 | **Normannognathus**
Jurassic Period

160 | **Aralazhdarcho**
Jurassic Period

114 | **Plataleorhynchus**
Late Jurassic or Early Cretaceous Period

72 | **Longchengpterus**
Cretaceous Period

74 | **Nurhachius**
Cretaceous Period

76 | **Coloborhynchus**
Cretaceous Period

78 | **Brasileodactylus**
Cretaceous Period

80 | **Istiodactylus**
Cretaceous Period

82 | **Anhanguera**
Cretaceous Period

84 | **Ornithocheirus**
Cretaceous Period

86 | **Haopterus**
Cretaceous Period

88 | **Uktenadactylus**
Cretaceous Period

90 | **Caulkicephalus**
Cretaceous Period

92 | **Ludodactylus**
Cretaceous Period

94 | **Pteranodon**
Cretaceous Period

96 | **Boreopterus**
Cretaceous Period

98 | **Feilongus**
Cretaceous Period

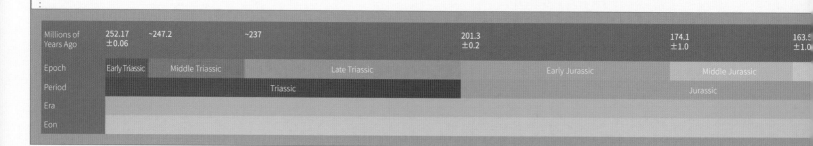

Millions of Years Ago	252.17 ±0.06	~247.2	~237		201.3 ±0.2		174.1 ±1.0	163.5 ±1.0
Epoch	Early Triassic	Middle Triassic	Late Triassic		Early Jurassic		Middle Jurassic	
Period			Triassic				Jurassic	
Era								
Eon								

100	*Nyctosaurus* Cretaceous Period
102	*Dawndraco* Cretaceous Period
104	*Zhenyuanopterus* Cretaceous Period
108	*Unwindia* Cretaceous Period
110	*Pterodaustro* Cretaceous Period
112	*Pterofiltrus* Cretaceous Period
116	*Cearadactylus* Cretaceous Period
118	*Gegepterus* Cretaceous Period
120	*Elanodactylus* Cretaceous Period
122	*Ningchengopterus* Cretaceous Period
128	*Nemicolopterus* Cretaceous Period
130	*Domeykodactylus* Cretaceous Period
138	*Dsungaripterus* Cretaceous Period
142	*Noripterus* Cretaceous Period

144	*Lonchognathosaurus* Cretaceous Period
146	*Phobetor* Cretaceous Period
148	*Hatzegopteryx* Cretaceous Period
150	*Eopteranodon* Cretaceous Period
152	*Azhdarcho* Cretaceous Period
154	*Shenzhoupterus* Cretaceous Period
156	*Tupandactylus* Cretaceous Period
158	*Tupuxuara* Cretaceous Period
162	*Quetzalcoatlus* Cretaceous Period

~145.0 100.5 66.0

Late Jurassic

Early Cretaceous

Late Cretaceous

Cretaceous

Mesozoic

Phanerozoic Eon

Archaeoistiodactylus

More ancient than an *Istiodactylus*

More ancient than the *Istiodactylus*, *Archaeoistiodactylus* was the earliest member of the *Istiodactylidae* family, which lived in the Middle Jurassic period.

The *Archaeoistiodactylus* fossil was preserved on a slab. It had missing parts, but the piece was good enough to show its distinctive features.

Archaeoistiodactylus and *Istiodactylus* looked similar. Both were medium-sized, had slender heads, small eyes, and sharp teeth in the front of their mouths.

Archaeoistiodactylus

Body size: Wingspan of about 2 meters
Diet: Fish
Period of existence: Cretaceous
Fossil origin: China, Asia

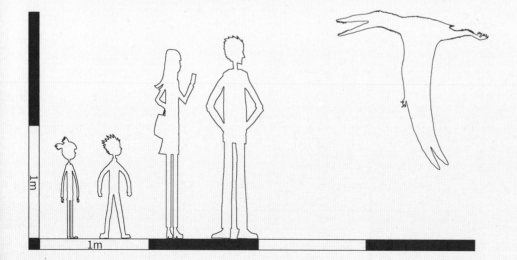

Longchengpterus
Close relative of *Nurhachius*

Longchengpterus was a good relative of *Nurhachius*. Both had a narrow and long head, as well as sharp teeth in the front of the mouth for catching fish. The difference was that *Longchengpterus* was smaller and had fewer teeth.

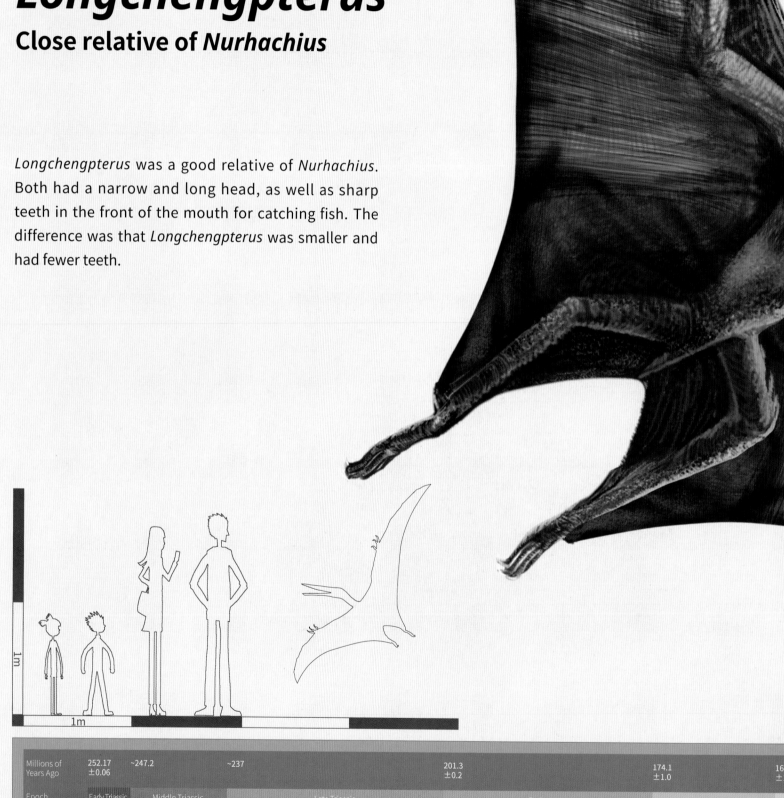

Millions of Years Ago	252.17 ±0.06	~247.2	~237		201.3 ±0.2		174.1 ±1.0	163.5 ±1.0
Epoch	Early Triassic	Middle Triassic		Late Triassic		Early Jurassic		Middle Jurassic
Period			Triassic				Jurassic	
Era								
Eon								

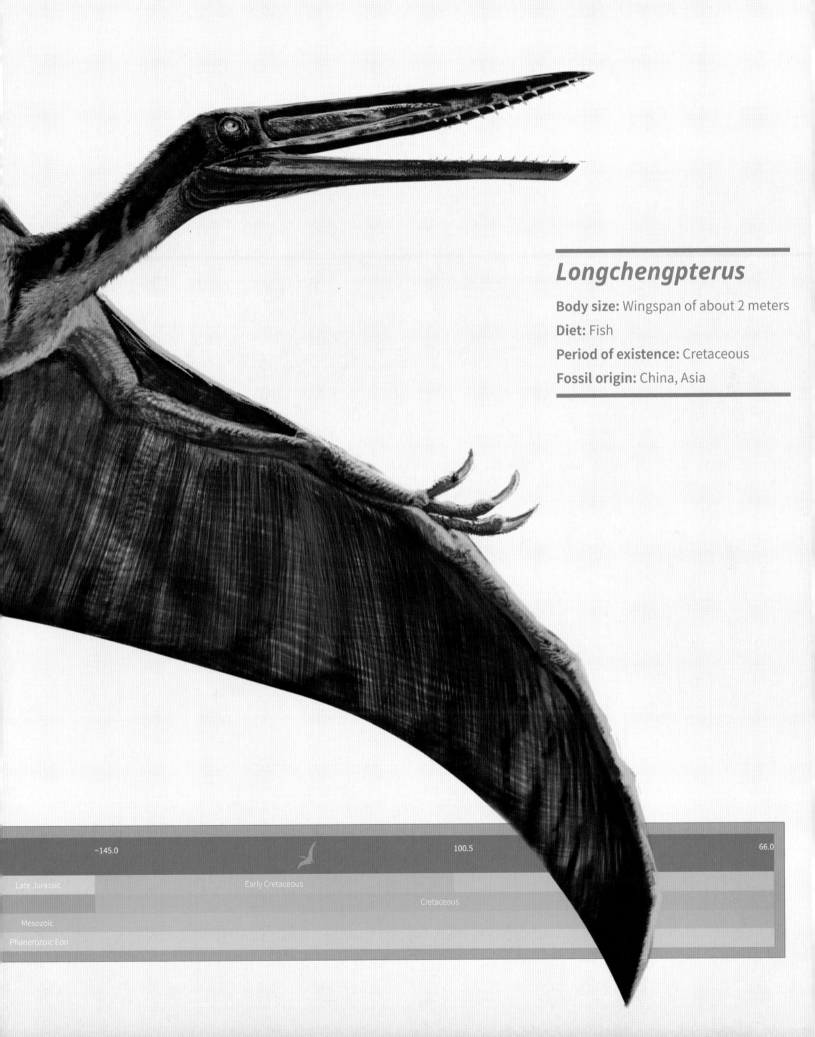

Longchengpterus

Body size: Wingspan of about 2 meters
Diet: Fish
Period of existence: Cretaceous
Fossil origin: China, Asia

~145.0   100.5   66.0

Late Jurassic   Early Cretaceous

Cretaceous

Mesozoic

Phanerozoic Eon

Nurhachius

Named after Nurhachi

Nurhachius was named after Nurhachi, the founder of a Chinese dynasty.

    Nurhachius had a huge head, which was almost one-third the length of its body. The big head was more than just for display. It was a good hunting tool and could steer in flying.

Nurhachius

Body size: Wingspan of 2–4 meters

Diet: Fish

Period of existence: Cretaceous

Fossil origin: China, Asia

1m

1m

Coloborhynchus

Lived in peace with the ferocious *Austroraptor*

In the Early Cretaceous period, the giant *Coloborhynchus* and ferocious *Austroraptor* lived together in the jungles of what would become South America. The hegemon of the sky and the overlord on land lived in peace.

This *Coloborhynchus* had a peaceful life and died without any complications. In the competitive environment at the time, a peaceful death was rare.

Coloborhynchus

Body size: Wingspan of 4–6 meters

Diet: Carnivorous

Period of existence: Cretaceous

Fossil origin: South America and Europe

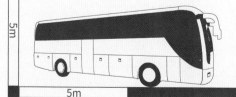

5m

5m

Brasileodactylus
from South America

Pterosaurs, flying in the sky, could easily snatch lizards from trees and fish from the water. But they could not win every single fight. Once landed, they would become much worse fighters. Look at that *Brasileodactylus*. This large pterosaur had a wingspan of up to four meters, but it was caught by an *Irritator*! So, even flyers could not afford to be complacent!

Brasileodactylus

Body size: Wingspan of about 4 meters
Diet: Fish
Period of existence: Cretaceous
Fossil origin: Brazil, South America

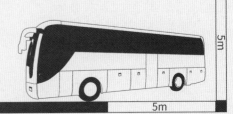

5m

5m

The strange
Istiodactylus

Most members of the *Istiodactylus* family had a duck-like mouth, which was flat and semicircular, and they were popularly called "duck-billed pterosaurs." But *Istiodactylus sinensis*, with a pointed and sharp-looking mouth, was an exception.

Some scientists thought that *Istiodactylus sinensis* and *Nurhachius* were the same species. If that was true, the *Istiodactylidae* family would include *Istiodactylus latidens* only, which were found in Europe.

Istiodactylus

Body size: Wingspan of about 2.7–5 meters
Diet: Fish
Period of existence: Cretaceous
Fossil origin: Asia and Europe

An *Anhanguera*
escaping before the battle

A *Maxakalisaurus*, an herbivorous dinosaur, was accidentally trapped in a swamp, and two *Armadillosuchus* followed its smell, ready to get an easy kill.

A resting *Anhanguera* saw this and took off immediately. It did not want to be part of this bloody battle.

The distinctive feature of the *Anhanguera* was that it had beautiful semicircular crests on both its upper and lower jaws. Their mouths were full of curved, conical teeth, perfect for fishing.

Anhanguera

Body size: Wingspan 4–4.5 meters

Diet: Fish

Period of existence: Cretaceous

Fossil origin: South America, Europe, and Oceania

5m

5m

Ornithocheirus
Flying to the other side of the sea

An *Ornithocheirus* looked sternly at the other side of the sea. It was its first trip to lay eggs there. Although feeling uneasy, it was encouraged by friends who had tried before. It felt that it could do this. Together they spread their wings, with the setting sun shining golden rays on them.

 Ornithocheirus, with a maximum wingspan of six meters, was the first large pterosaur. Their jaws were straight, and their upper and lower jaws had semicircular crests.

Ornithocheirus

Body size: Wingspan up to 6 meters

Diet: Fish

Period of existence: Cretaceous

Fossil origin: Europe and South America

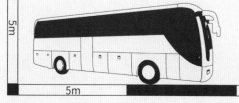

5m

5m

Haopterus

Where's my fish?

If it did not drop the fish accidentally, *Haopterus* would never walk about on land. It was an excellent flyer, but on land, it walked terribly like a toddler. It was so slow!

    Haopterus was not big. If they had to walk on land, they did so on four feet. Their heads were long and low, with no crest.

Haopterus

Body size: Wingspan up to 1.35 meters
Diet: Fish
Period of existence: Cretaceous
Fossil origin: China, Asia

1m

1m

Uktenadactylus

Were they related to a horned snake?

The mysterious name of the *Uktenadactylus* meant "horned snake" and came from a myth of the Cherokees, a North American tribe.

The *Uktenadactylus* had a large wingspan and a small body. They had distinct crests, sharp teeth in their mouths, and looked remarkably like the *Anhanguera*.

Uktenadactylus

Body size: Wingspan of about 5 meters
Diet: Fish
Period of existence: Cretaceous
Fossil origin: United States, North America

5m

Millions of Years Ago	252.17 ±0.06	~247.2	~237		201.3 ±0.2		174.1 ±1.0	163.5 ±1.0
Epoch	Early Triassic	Middle Triassic	Late Triassic			Early Jurassic	Middle Jurassic	
Period			Triassic				Jurassic	
Era								
Eon								

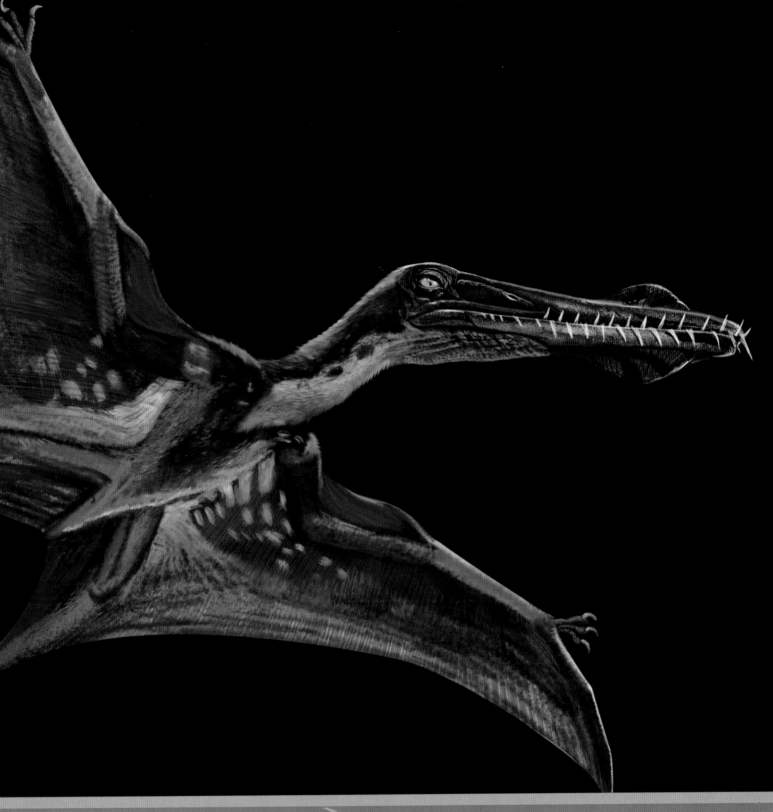

~145.0

100.5

66.0

Late Jurassic

Early Cretaceous

Late Cretaceous

Cretaceous

Mesozoic

Phanerozoic Eon

Caulkicephalus
frightens away a drinking *Ampelosaurus*

In the Early Cretaceous period, in present-day Europe, a *Caulkicephalus*, showing off its ornate crest, skimmed over the water. With sharp teeth extending out of its mouth and long wings fanning ripples, the pterosaur looked terrifying. An *Ampelosaurus*, which was about to drink water, turned around and walked to the forest, hoping to drink safely only after the big guy had flown over.

Caulkicephalus had large, pointed teeth in the front part of its mouth, smaller ones in the middle, and bigger ones at the back. Its fishing tool was the smaller ones in the middle, which could snatch fish easily.

Caulkicephalus

Body size: Wingspan of about 4 meters
Diet: Fish
Period of existence: Cretaceous
Fossil origin: United Kingdom, Europe

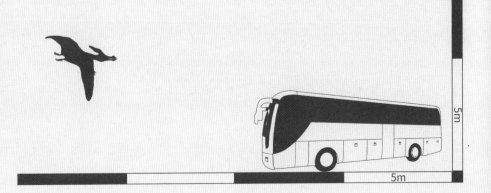

5m

5m

Ludodactylus
Not as cute as its name

The name of *Ludodactylus* meant "toy," but in fact, this pterosaur was not as cute as one. As it opened its mouth, showing sharp fangs and eyes glittering greedily at its prey, it was nothing less than a bloodthirsty killer.

Unlike other *Ornithocheiridae* pterosaurs, *Ludodactylus*'s crest was not on the maxillary, but instead on the back of its head.

Ludodactylus

Body size: Wingspan of about 5 meters
Diet: Fish
Period of existence: Cretaceous
Fossil origin: Brazil, South America

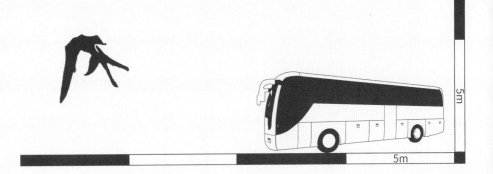

5m

5m

Pteranodon

Admire my crest!

The sun was setting, and the whole world was basking in a colorful hue. A female *Pteranodon* seemed to be attracted by the gorgeous view. It stood on the top of a hill and looked quietly at the rosy sky.

Its lover felt somewhat ignored. It flew in front of the female's eyes, showing off its crest in the evening sun's glow.

With a wingspan of more than seven meters, the *Pteranodon* was one of the largest pterosaurs. Its distinctive feature was its toothless beak, similar to today's birds.

Pteranodon

Body size: Wingspan more than 7 meters

Diet: Carnivorous

Period of existence: Cretaceous

Fossil origin: United States, North America

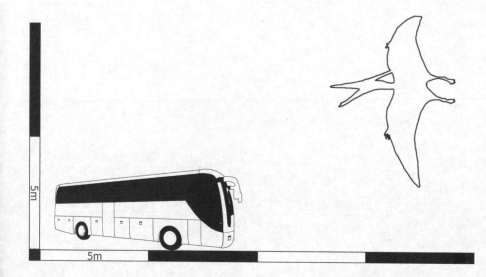

5m

5m

Boreopterus
Light and flexible glider

In the Early Cretaceous period, in present-day northeastern China, a *Boreopterus* landed softly on a magical-looking tree.

Flying over a foggy river, it tried to find some food.

Paleontologists speculated that the small *Boreopterus* were light and flexible gliders, like today's frigatebirds.

Boreopterus

Body size: Wingspan of about 1.5 meters
Diet: Fish
Period of existence: Cretaceous
Fossil origin: China, Asia

1m

1m

A *Feilongus*

hiding in the rain

A pterosaur was flying home moments before a storm. Its name *Feilongus* was Chinese, meaning the legendary "flying dragon."

The most unusual part of the *Feilongus* was that it had two crests, with the lower one on its back and the other extending backward on the back of the skull. The *Feilongus* was of medium size and good at gliding.

Feilongus

Body size: Wingspan of about 2.4 meters
Diet: Fish
Period of existence: Cretaceous
Fossil origin: China, Asia

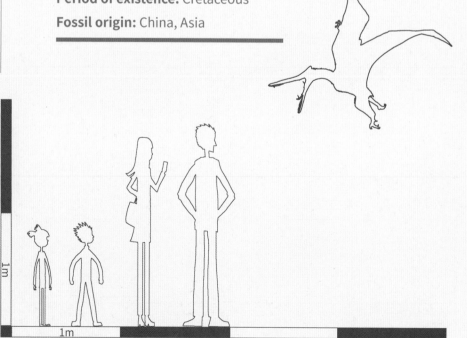

Nyctosaurus
flew majestically across the sky

Dusk makes all animals homesick. As the warm hue enveloped Earth, a group of *Nyctosaurus* finished a day of hunting and started to go home.

In the vast sky, these *Nyctosaurus* were prominent. Their large towering crests and wide wings looked like gigantic aircraft.

Nyctosaurus was the only pterosaur that lacked claws on its forelimbs, so it could climb neither rocks nor trees. It spent most of its time in flight.

Nyctosaurus

Body size: Wingspan of 2 meters
Diet: Carnivorous
Period of existence: Cretaceous
Fossil origin: United States, North America

Reconstructed model of Sail the *Nyctosaurus*

The toothless
Dawndraco

Dawndraco had a large mouth but no teeth. The feature did not make its hunting more difficult, but instead, it reduced the weight of its skull. Its streamlined head made flight easier.

The *Dawndraco* had a small body, a large wingspan, and a slightly raised crest at the back of the head. It looked like it was elegantly wearing a small hat.

Dawndraco

Body size: Wingspan of about 5 meters
Diet: Fish
Period of existence: Cretaceous
Fossil origin: United States, North America

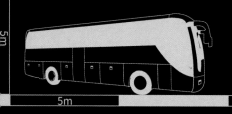

5m

5m

Millions of Years Ago	252.17 ±0.06	~247.2		~237		201.3 ±0.2		174.1 ±1.0	163. ±1.
Epoch	Early Triassic	Middle Triassic			Late Triassic		Early Jurassic	Middle Jurassic	
Period			Triassic					Jurassic	
Era									
Eon									

~145.0

100.5

66.0

Late Jurassic

Early Cretaceous

Late Cretaceous

Cretaceous

Mesozoic

Phanerozoic Eon

The large-headed
Zhenyuanopterus

The distinctive feature of the *Zhenyuan-opterus* was its half-meter long head, which had a low, irregular-shaped crest. It had numerous staggered teeth, which made it look terrifying.

Zhenyuanopterus lived near lakes and often flew low above the water to fish.

Zhenyuanopterus

Body size: Wingspan of about 4 meters
Diet: Fish
Period of existence: Cretaceous
Fossil origin: China, Asia

1m

1m

Ctenochasma

With a mouth like a funnel and teeth like a comb

The early morning sun shone through leaves onto a plain in the Late Jurassic period, in what would later become Central Europe. The clear lake's ripples reflected sunlight. As the light drove the darkness away, animals in a nearby forest started to get up from their slumber.

Two *Ctenochasma* stepped into the pond to enjoy the cool water. They had nearly four hundred needle-like teeth. While not strong enough to tear the flesh of their prey apart, they could work as a funnel to trap many fish in their mouths. Then, they could simply filter out the water, and what remained would be a great meal! This fishing method greatly increased their efficiency and success rate. And the fish knew it, too, so when they saw this "funnel" appearing, they would hide as far away as possible.

Ctenochasma

Body size: Wingspan of 0.25–1.2 meters
Diet: Fish
Period of existence: Jurassic
Fossil origin: Germany and France, Europe

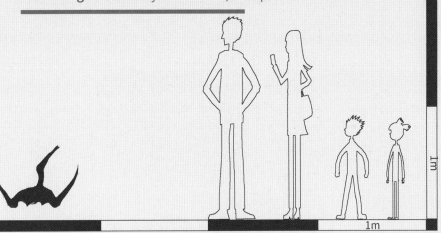

Armed with "pincers"
Unwindia

Unwindia was discovered in 2011, with its fossil found in a small town outside the city of Cariri, in the northeastern Brazilian state of Ceará. The most obvious feature of *Unwindia* was its sharp, uneven teeth, which looked like pincers used to catch fish.

Millions of Years Ago	252.17 ±0.06	~247.2	~237		201.3 ±0.2		174.1 ±1.0	163.5 ±1.0
Epoch	Early Triassic	Middle Triassic	Late Triassic			Early Jurassic	Middle Jurassic	
Period			Triassic				Jurassic	
Era								
Eon								

Unwindia

Body size: Wingspan of about 2 meters
Diet: Fish
Period of existence: Cretaceous
Fossil origin: Brazil, South America

~145.0   100.5   66.0

Late Jurassic   Early Cretaceous   Late Cretaceous

Cretaceous

Mesozoic

Phanerozoic Eon

Pterodaustro
Taking in fish in big gulps

As the morning sun shone through the leaves on the lake, the whole forest was enveloped in lovely light.

Two *Pterodaustro* met to fish together. This was their way of having a great time with friends.

Pterodaustro stood in the water and put their long mouths under. Why, you may ask, didn't they act like other pterosaurs, flying low over the water to fish? The reason was their teeth. They had more than one thousand teeth, twenty-four per centimeter on their jaws. The many teeth made a different way of fishing possible. They did not aim and catch. Instead, they scoop up fish, crustaceans, and plankton as if using a ladle.

Pterodaustro

Body size: Wingspan of about 1.33 meters
Diet: Fish and plankton
Period of existence: Cretaceous
Fossil origin: Argentina and Chile, South America

A hunting
Pterofiltrus

Look at the mouth of those *Pterofiltrus*, which were about to fish in direct sunlight. Like *Ctenochasma*, they would stick their long mouths into water, wait for fish to swim inside, close the mouth, filter the water out, then swallow the fish. Both *Pterofiltrus* and *Ctenochasma* belong to the *Ctenochasmatidae* family, which was one of the most dominant pterosaur groups in the Jehol Biota, the Lower Cretaceous ecosystem of northeastern China.

Pterofiltrus

Body size: Wingspan of about 1.5 meters
Diet: Fish
Period of existence: Cretaceous
Fossil origin: China, Asia

1m

Plataleorhynchus

A dancer on water

A white *Plataleorhynchus* landed from the air. It was flying low, with its round mouth touching the surface of the water, making beautiful ripples. It was skimming the lake gracefully as if it was dancing.

But you probably did not expect chaos underneath, as the fish were running for their lives.

Plataleorhynchus was not dancing; its semicircular, sickle-like mouth was sweeping back and forth in the water, stirring up mud and waterweed to get the aquatic animals out, so it could eat them.

Plataleorhynchus

Body size: Wingspan of about 2 meters

Diet: Fish

Period of existence: Late Jurassic or Early Cretaceous

Fossil origin: United Kingdom, Europe

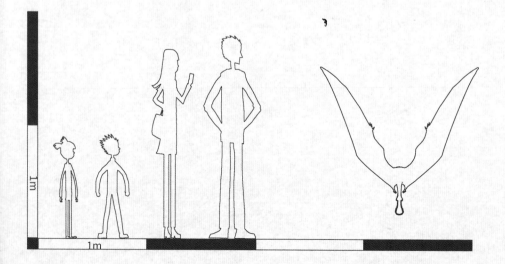

Cearadactylus
A cruel predator

The species of *Cearadactylus* is *C. atrox*, meaning "fierce," because scientists found its terrifying teeth fossil impressive. *Cearadactylus* had long, sharp teeth like steel spikes, which could capture marine animals with ease.

    Cearadactylus was large, but unlike many large gliders, it could power its flight by flapping its wings.

Cearadactylus

Body size: Wingspan of 4–5.5 meters

Diet: Fish

Period of existence: Cretaceous

Fossil origin: Brazil, South America

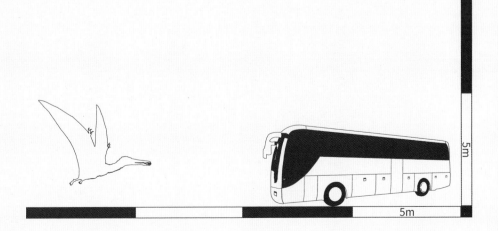

Gegepterus
An aristocratic pterosaur

"Gege" is a Manchu term for aristocratic women, and one pterosaur was named as such—the *Gegepterus*. It was named so because its fossils were carefully preserved, in the same way a lady would carefully look after her appearance.

The small *Gegepterus* had a long beak and needle-like teeth.

Gegepterus

Body size: Wingspan of about 1.5 meters
Diet: Fish
Period of existence: Cretaceous
Fossil origin: China, Asia

Elanodactylus

Dive attack like a kite

A kite is a small member of the *Accipitridae* (hawk) family. They are naturally ferocious and great at soaring for a long time in the sky. *Elanodactylus*'s name meant "kite finger," and scientists speculate that it may also be as fierce as a kite, often swooping down from the air to attack.

Elanodactylus was medium-sized, with a long head and dense, sharp teeth in the front of its beak.

Elanodactylus

Body size: Wingspan of about 2.5 meters

Diet: Fish

Period of existence: Cretaceous

Fossil origin: China, Asia

Ningchengopterus
A fluffy child

In excavating the fossils of *Ningchengopterus*, scientists found an almost-complete skeleton of a juvenile, including the usually hard-to-preserve wing membrane and soft tissues of hair. This precious fossil provides clues for scientists, who identified that *Ningchengopterus* was covered in a thin coat of fluff.

Therefore, the reconstructed *Ningchengopterus* looked fluffy and cute!

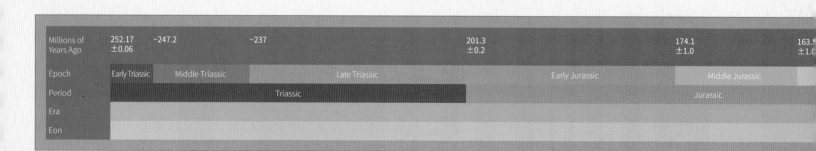

Millions of Years Ago	252.17 ±0.06	~247.2		~237			201.3 ±0.2		174.1 ±1.0	163.5 ±1.0
Epoch	Early Triassic	Middle Triassic			Late Triassic			Early Jurassic		Middle Jurassic
Period				Triassic					Jurassic	
Era										
Eon										

Ningchengopterus

Body size: Wingspan greater than 0.5 meters
Diet: Fish
Period of existence: Cretaceous
Fossil origin: China, Asia

1m

1m

~145.0

100.5

66.0

Late Jurassic

Early Cretaceous

Late Cretaceous

Cretaceous

Mesozoic

Phanerozoic Eon

Pterodactylus
The food sharer

An unlucky three-meter-long *Proceratosaurus* went to a pond in the valley for a drink but was attacked. The predator had their meal and left the carcass of the *Proceratosaurus* behind. This excited the *Pterodactylus* hovering over the dead body. They usually ate fish, but it would be nice to try meat occasionally. They tore the flesh of the prey with sharp teeth, making the air around them bloody.

Pterodactylus

Body size: Wingspan of about 1.5 meters

Diet: Carnivorous

Period of existence: Jurassic

Fossil origin: Germany, Europe

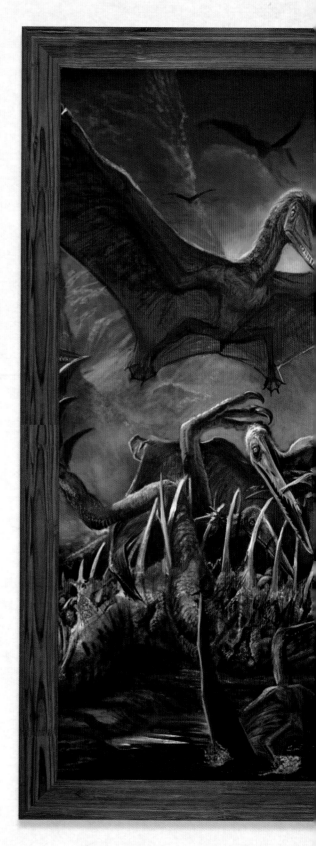

Tendaguripterus
Flying over present-day Africa

In the early 1920s, people found a large number of dinosaurs and pterosaurs in Tendaguru, Tanzania, Africa. Scientists unearthed a total of 250 tons of fossils, which filled more than one thousand large wooden crates. Among the discovery was *Tendaguripterus*, the first pterosaur found in the area.

1m

1m

Millions of Years Ago	252.17 ±0.06	~247.2		~237		201.3 ±0.2		174.1 ±1.0		163.5 ±1.0
Epoch	Early Triassic	Middle Triassic			Late Triassic		Early Jurassic		Middle Jurassic	
Period			Triassic					Jurassic		
Era										
Eon										

Tendaguripterus

Body size: Wingspan of less than 1 meter
Food: Shellfish or crabs
Period of existence: Jurassic
Fossil origin: Tanzania, Africa

~145.0   100.5   66.0

Late Jurassic   Early Cretaceous

Cretaceous   Cretaceous

Mesozoic

Phanerozoic Eon

Nemicolopterus
As big as a sparrow

The *Nemicolopterus*, which lived in present-day northeastern China during the Early Cretaceous period, was as cute as a sparrow because it was only nine centimeters long. However, some researchers suggested that it was small because the fossil belonged to a juvenile.

Most pterosaur fossils were found in marine sediments, suggesting that they lived near the sea and loved to eat fish. The *Nemicolopterus*, however, lived inland and liked to stay on top of trees and eat insects.

Nemicolopterus

Body size: Wingspan of about 0.25 meters
Diet: Insects
Period of existence: Cretaceous
Fossil origin: China, Asia

5cm

5cm

**Reconstructed model of
Tracy the *Nemicolopterus***

Millions of Years Ago	252.17 ±0.06	~247.2	~237		201.3 ±0.2	174.1 ±1.0
Epoch	Early Triassic	Middle Triassic	Late Triassic		Early Jurassic	Middle Jurass
Period			Triassic		Jurassic	
Era						
Eon						

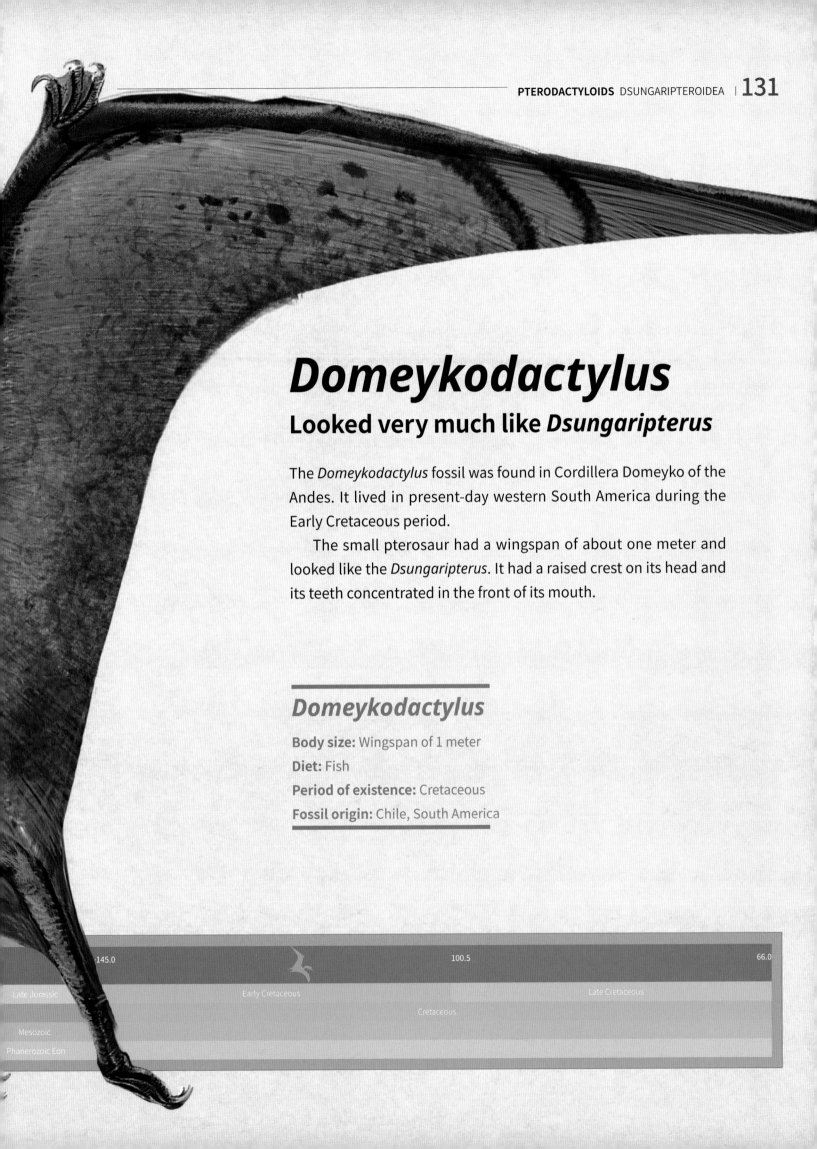

Domeykodactylus
Looked very much like *Dsungaripterus*

The *Domeykodactylus* fossil was found in Cordillera Domeyko of the Andes. It lived in present-day western South America during the Early Cretaceous period.

The small pterosaur had a wingspan of about one meter and looked like the *Dsungaripterus*. It had a raised crest on its head and its teeth concentrated in the front of its mouth.

Domeykodactylus

Body size: Wingspan of 1 meter
Diet: Fish
Period of existence: Cretaceous
Fossil origin: Chile, South America

145.0	100.5	66.0
Late Jurassic	Early Cretaceous	Late Cretaceous
	Cretaceous	
Mesozoic		
Phanerozoic Eon		

The happy lives of the
Herbstosaurus &
Piatnitzkysaurus

When the *Herbstosaurus* was first discovered, it was thought to be a dinosaur—one of the smallest because it was so tiny. *Herbstosaurus*'s fossils are so limited that one can only guess what it looked like based on its close relatives.

   Herbstosaurus lived in the same region as the *Piatnitzkysaurus*, a large, ferocious carnivorous dinosaur. Even so, they could live in peace and even chatted amicably because they each held their own territory and had no intention of invading the other's.

Herbstosaurus

Body size: Wingspan of less than 1 meter
Diet: Carnivorous
Period of existence: Jurassic
Fossil origin: Argentina, South America

Altmuehlopterus
Used to be called *Daitingopterus*

Altmuehlopterus's fossil was found early, but it got its name only in 2017. Before that, it used to have an unofficial name, *Daitingopterus*, and Chinese paleontologists took the liberty to translate its name into "Dante pterosaur," the same name as the Renaissance poet.

The small *Altmuehlopterus* had a large wingspan and a large head with sharp teeth in its mouth.

Altmuehlopterus

Body size: Wingspan of 1.08 meters
Diet: Fish
Period of existence: Jurassic
Fossil origin: Germany, Europe

Germanodactylus

Body size: Wingspan of 0.98–1.08 meters

Diet: Fish

Period of existence: Jurassic

Fossil origin: Germany, Europe

1m

1m

Millions of Years Ago	252.17 ±0.06	~247.2	~237			201.3 ±0.2	
Epoch	Early Triassic	Middle Triassic		Late Triassic			
Period			Triassic				Jurassic
Era							
Eon							

Germanodactylus
Too ordinary

The *Germanodactylus* was so common that scientists could not decide which family to place it into. Thus, it was once classified into the *Germanodactylidae* family, later in the *Dsungaripteroidea* superfamily, and was once considered to be a juvenile *Pterodactylus* or *Pterodactylus*'s close relative. It wasn't until 2006 that the controversy was settled.

    Germanodactylus was small. It had a low crest on its head and a sharp beak.

~145.0   100.5   66.0

Early Cretaceous   Late Cretaceous

Cretaceous

Mesozoic

Phanerozoic Eon

Dsungaripterus
with long and curved jaws

Dsungaripterus had a large extended family. Their fossils were first found in the Junggar Basin in Xinjiang, China, and later in remote Africa. *Dsungaripterus* liked to catch shellfish and worms from sandy mudflats, and they could do so because of their long, curved jaws.

Dsungaripterus

Body size: Wingspan of 3–5 meters

Diet: Shellfish and insects

Period of existence: Cretaceous

Fossil origin: Asia and Africa

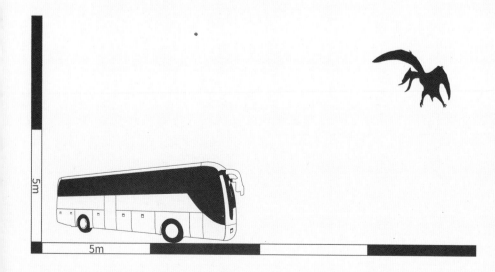

5m

5m

The lizard-eating
Normannognathus

Fossils of the *Normannognathus* were found in marine sediments, suggesting that it should have lived and fed on fish. But scientists found that its teeth were large, unlike those of fish-eating pterosaurs. So they hypothesized that *Normannognathus* might attack small land animals, such as lizards.

1m

1m

Millions of Years Ago	252.17 ±0.06	~247.2	~237		201.3 ±0.2
Epoch	Early Triassic	Middle Triassic		Late Triassic	
Period			Triassic		
Era					
Eon					

Normannognathus

Body size: Wingspan of 1 meter
Diet: Fish or small animals
Period of existence: Jurassic
Fossil origin: France, Europe

100.5

66.0

Early Cretaceous

Late Cretaceous

Late Jurassic

Cretaceous

Mesozoic

Phanerozoic Eon

Noripterus

A dancer on the lake

Noripterus lived near lakes; therefore, paleontologists gave them a name that means "lake wings."

Noripterus lived in the Early Cretaceous period in present-day Xinjiang, China. It had a large, pointed head with a long, narrow bony crest. Two rows of sharp teeth grew in the mouth of the *Noripterus*. These teeth were sharp enough to easily crush the hard shells of its prey.

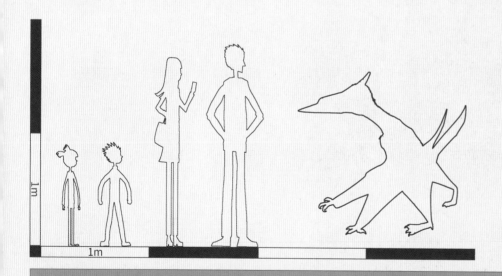

1m

1m

Millions of Years Ago	252.17 ±0.06	~247.2		~237		201.3 ±0.2		174.1 ±1.0
Epoch	Early Triassic	Middle Triassic			Late Triassic		Early Jurassic	Middle Jurassic
Period				Triassic				Jurassic
Era								
Eon								

Noripterus

Body size: Wingspan of up to 4 meters

Diet: Fish and shellfish

Period of existence: Cretaceous

Fossil origin: China, Asia

~145.0

100.5

66.0

Late Jurassic

Early Cretaceous

Late Cretaceous

Phan

Lonchognathosaurus
had a spear-like mouth

Remember the aforementioned *Dorygnathus*, the guy with a spear-like mouth? Now, let's meet another one, the *Lonchognathosaurus*, which also had a spear-like mouth. Most pterosaurs had curved lower maxillary, but the *Lonchognathosaurus* had a straight jaw that looked like a spear or lance. Although it looked like *Dorygnathus*, it was a different genus. The *Dorygnathus* lived in Early Jurassic times, in present-day Europe, while the *Lonchognathosaurus* lived in the Early Cretaceous period, in present-day Xinjiang, China.

Lonchognathosaurus

Body size: Wingspan of about 4 meters
Diet: Fish
Period of existence: Cretaceous
Fossil origin: China, Asia

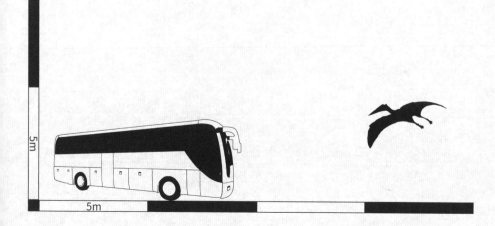

5m

5m

Phobetor
Possibly nonexistent

Phobetor was named by paleontologists based on the "frightener" in Greek mythology, meaning that this pterosaur could terrify the inhabitants on land.

The legendary and powerful name was unfortunately invalid because it was taken by a fish species before paleontologists put it on this pterosaur. Under the rules of binomial nomenclature, *Phobetor* needed another name.

But something sad happened before its naming. Researchers studied its fossil again and found it was probably the same as *Noripterus*. So *Phobetor* might not have been existent as a distinct genus.

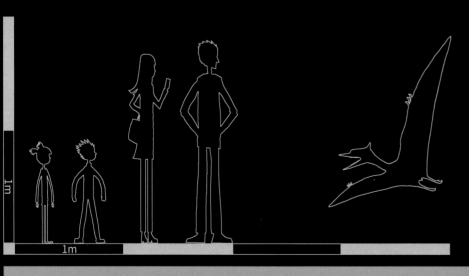

1m

Millions of Years Ago	252.17 ±0.06	~247.2	~237		201.3 ±0.2		174.1 ±1.0	163.5 ±1.0
Epoch	Early Triassic	Middle Triassic	Late Triassic			Early Jurassic	Middle Jurassic	
Period			Triassic				Jurassic	
Era								
Eon								

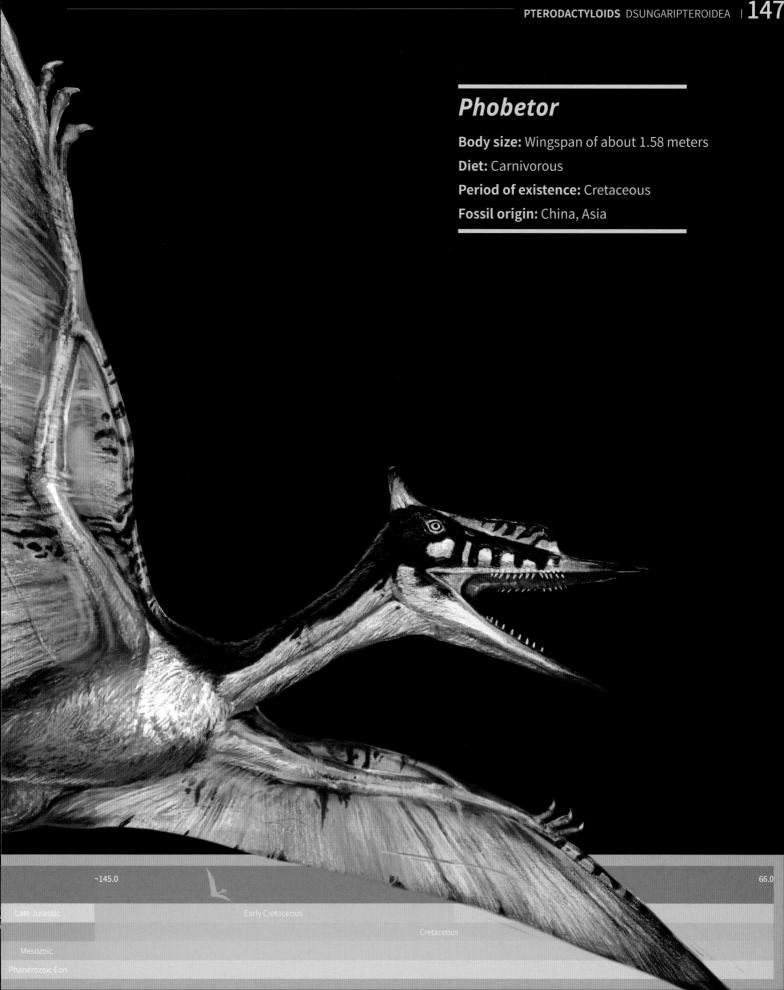

Phobetor

Body size: Wingspan of about 1.58 meters

Diet: Carnivorous

Period of existence: Cretaceous

Fossil origin: China, Asia

~145.0

66.0

Late Jurassic

Early Cretaceous

Cretaceous

Mesozoic

Phanerozoic Eon

Hatzegopteryx
A giant from Romania

5m

5m

Millions of Years Ago	252.17 ±0.06	~247.2	~237		201.3 ±0.2		174.1 ±1.0	163.5 ±1.0
Epoch	Early Triassic	Middle Triassic	Late Triassic			Early Jurassic	Middle Jurassic	
Period			Triassic				Jurassic	
Era								
Eon								

Hatzegopteryx thambema, which was from present-day Romania, had its specific name meaning "monster" because scientists think that word is appropriate for this giant.

With a head of about three meters, a standing height of five meters, and a wingspan of up to twelve meters,

Hatzegopteryx was probably the world's largest pterosaur ever, larger than the *Quetzalcoatlus*. However, some researchers disagree, arguing that the *Hatzegopteryx*'s humerus was distorted during preservation, exaggerating its length, so its wingspan could be smaller than that of the *Quetzalcoatlu*s.

Hatzegopteryx

Body size: Wingspan up to 12 meters

Diet: Carnivorous

Period of existence: Cretaceous

Fossil origin: Romania, Europe

~145.0   100.5   66.0

Late Jurassic   Early Cretaceous   Late Cretaceous

Cretaceous

Mesozoic

Phanerozoic Eon

Eopteranodon
More primitive than the *Pteranodon*

Eopteranodon was a more primitive genus than the *Pteranodon*. It had a large, crested head, a long neck, and large wings. Because of its smaller size, it always fed on small fish, shrimp, or insects, and was far less terrifying than other pterosaurs who lived in western Liaoning Province, China.

Eopteranodon

Body size: Wingspan of about 1.1 meters

Diet: Carnivorous

Period of existence: Cretaceous

Fossil origin: China, Asia

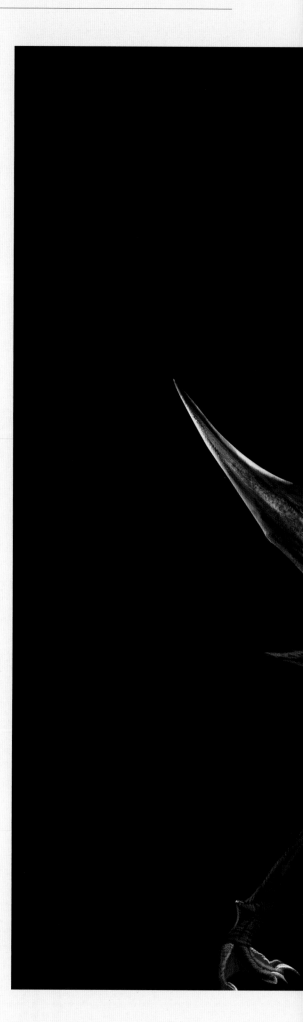

Azhdarcho

Body size: Wingspan of about 6 meters

Diet: Carnivorous

Period of existence: Cretaceous

Fossil origin: Uzbekistan, Asia

5m

Millions of Years Ago	252.17 ±0.06	~247.2		~237				174.1 ±1.0	163.5 ±1.0
Epoch	Early Triassic	Middle Triassic			Late Triassic			Early Jurassic	Middle Jurassic
Period				Triassic				Jurassic	
Era									
Eon									

Azhdarcho
A cruel killer from above

Although *Azhdarcho* had no teeth, its long and pointed jaws were deadly. It was an excellent flyer and a ruthless aerial killer that could attack from high places to catch prey in the water, on the ground, or even in the sky.

~145.0   100.5   66.0

Late Jurassic   Early Cretaceous   Late Cretaceous

Cretaceous

Mesozoic

Phanerozoic Eon

Small, large-headed, toothless
Shenzhoupterus

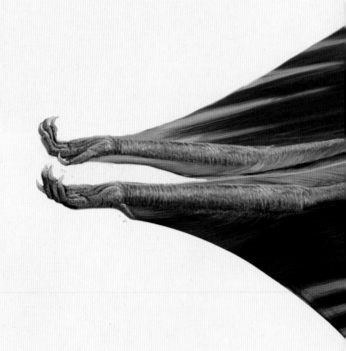

Living in the Early Cretaceous period in present-day northeastern China, the *Shenzhoupterus* was the smallest member of the *Chaoyangopteridae* family. Despite its size, it had a disproportionately big head. The fossil showed that its skull was about twenty-five centimeters long and appeared to be larger than the rest of its body.

Shenzhoupterus had a long, pointed mouth with no teeth. Its crest extended from the top of its eyes to the back of the head, rising at the end.

1m

1m

Millions of Years Ago	252.17 ±0.06	~247.2	~237		201.3 ±0.2		174.1 ±1.0	163.5 ±1.0
Epoch	Early Triassic	Middle Triassic		Late Triassic		Early Jurassic		Middle Jurassic
Period			Triassic				Jurassic	
Era								
Eon								

Shenzhoupterus

Body size: Wingspan of 1.4 meters

Diet: Fish

Period of existence: Cretaceous

Fossil origin: China, Asia

100.5   66.0

Early Cretaceous   Late Cretaceous

Cretaceous

Tupandactylus
Sail-like crest

Tupandactylus's huge crest was distinctive. *Tupandactylus*'s skull was only about 0.15 meters thick, but the crest could grow to 1.2 meters, eight times as tall. The crest, like a ship's sail, rose high on its head.

The small *Tupandactylus* had narrow, long wings, like today's albatrosses. It often flew over the open sea, preying on marine fish.

Tupandactylus

Body size: Wingspan up to 6 meters
Diet: Fish
Period of existence: Cretaceous
Fossil origin: Brazil, South America

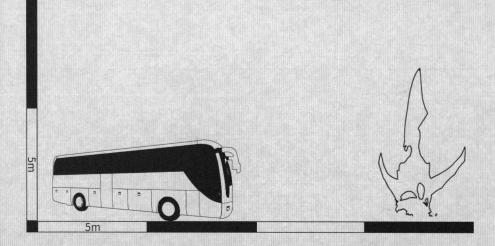

5m

5m

Familiar-spirit-like magical
Tupuxuara

Have you heard about the familiar spirits in European folklore? Are they magical? Now, I will show you a magical pterosaur!

When scientists discovered the *Tupuxuara*, they were amazed by its gorgeous crest, so they gave it a magical name. They believed that both male and female adults had beautiful crests with complex patterns. The difference was that the back of the female's crest was more rounded and looked less aggressive than the male's.

Tupuxuara

Body size: Wingspan of about 5.5 meters
Diet: Fish
Period of existence: Cretaceous
Fossil origin: Brazil, South America

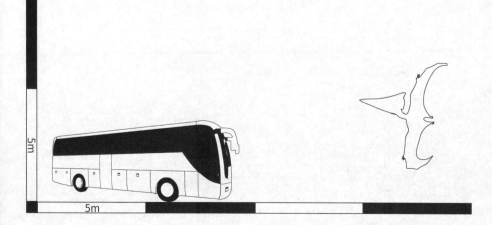

5m

5m

Aralazhdarcho

God of Sky in present-day Central Asia

Fossils of the *Aralazhdarcho* were found in Kazakhstan, Uzbekistan, and Tajikistan in Central Asia. It was one of the few pterosaurs that lived in present-day Central Asia. Its fossils were incomplete, so scientists could only speculate that it was a medium-sized or large pterosaur.

Aralazhdarcho

Body size: Unknown

Diet: Unknown

Period of existence: Jurassic

Fossil origin: Central Asia

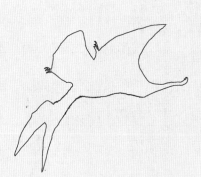

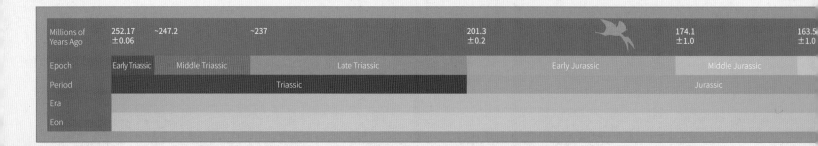

Millions of Years Ago	252.17 ±0.06	~247.2		~237		201.3 ±0.2		174.1 ±1.0	163.5 ±1.0
Epoch	Early Triassic	Middle Triassic		Late Triassic			Early Jurassic	Middle Jurassic	
Period			Triassic					Jurassic	
Era									
Eon									

~145.0		100.5		66.0
Late Jurassic	Early Cretaceous		Late Cretaceous	
		Cretaceous		
Mesozoic				
Phanerozoic Eon				

Quetzalcoatlus
The most famous pterosaur

Quetzalcoatlus was the most famous pterosaur, and for a long time, it was considered the largest. Their wingspans could reach twelve meters or even larger. Their heads and necks were nearly three meters. When they stood on the ground, they were more than five meters tall, like giraffes. In recent years, however, some researchers suggested that the *Hatzegopteryx* might be larger. Still, the *Quetzalcoatlus* was no doubt the dominator in the sky, and its glorious legend continued to be admired by us to this day.

Quetzalcoatlus

Body size: Wingspan up to 12 meters

Diet: Carnivorous

Period of existence: Cretaceous

Fossil origin: United States, North America

Index

References

1. Hone, David W. E., and Michael J. Benton. (2008). "A new genus of rhynchosaur from the Middle Triassic of south-west England." *Palaeontology* 51 (1): 95–115.

2. Keller, Thomas (1985). "Quarrying and Fossil Collecting in the Posidonienschiefer (Upper Liassic) around Holzmaden, Germany." *Geological Curator* 4(4): 193–198.

3. Andres, Brian, James M. Clark, and Xu Xing. (2010). "A new rhamphorhynchid pterosaur from the Upper Jurassic of Xinjiang, China, and the phylogenetic relationships of basal pterosaurs." *Journal of Vertebrate Paleontology* 30(1): 163–187.

4. Gasparini, Zulma, Marta Fernández, and Marcelo de la Fuente. (2004). "A new pterosaur from the Jurassic of Cuba." *Palaeontology* 47 (4): 919–927.

5. Colbert, Edwin H. (1969). "A Jurassic pterosaur from Cuba." *American Museum Novitates* 2370: 1–26 [2007-03-03].

6. Jensen, James A., and John H. Ostrom. (1977). "A second Jurassic pterosaur from North America." *Journal of Paleontology* 51 (4): 867–870.

7. Schmitz, L., and R. Motani. (2011). "Nocturnality in Dinosaurs Inferred from Scleral Ring and Orbit Morphology." *Science* 332.

8. Carpenter, K., D. M. Unwin, K. Cloward, C. A. Miles, and C. Miles. (2003). "A new scaphognathine pterosaur from the Upper Jurassic Formation of Wyoming, USA." *Geological Society of London* 217:45–54.

9. Xiaolin, Wang, Zhou Zhonghe, He Huaiyu, Jin Fan, Wang Yuanqing, Zhang Jiangyong, Wang Yuan, Xu Xing, and Zhang Fucheng. (2005). "Stratigraphy and age of the Daohugou Bed in Ningcheng, Inner Mongolia." *Chinese Science Bulletin* 50 (20): 2369–2376.

10. Lü, J., X. Fuchn, and J. Chen. (2010). "A new scaphognathine pterosaur from the Middle Jurassic of western Liaoning, China." *Acta Geoscientica Sinica* 31 (2): 263–266.

11. Osi, A. (2010). "Feeding-related characters in basal pterosaurs: implications for jaw mechanism, dental function and diet." *Lethaia*.

12. Dalla Vecchia, F. M. (1995). "A new pterosaur (Reptilia, Pterosauria) from the Norian (Late Triassic) of Friuli (Northeastern Italy), Preliminary note." *Gortania* 16: 59–66.

13. Jain, S. L. (1974)."Jurassic Pterosaur from India", *Journal of the Geological Society of India* 15 (3): 330–335.

14. Wang, X., A. W. A. Kellner, S. Jiang, and X. Meng. (2009). "An unusual long-tailed pterosaur with elongated neck from western Liaoning of China." *Anais da Academia Brasileira de Ciência* 81 (4): 793–812.

15. Fröbisch, N. B., and J. Fröbisch. (2006). "A new basal pterosaur genus from the upper Triassic of the Northern Calcareous Alps of Switzerland." *Palaeontology* 49 (5): 1081–1090.

16. Stecher, Rico. (2008). "A new Triassic pterosaur from Switzerland (Central Austroalpine, Grisons), *Raeticodactylus filisurensis* gen. et sp. Nov." *Swiss Journal of Geosciences* 101: 185.

17. Dalla Vecchia, F. M. (2009). "Anatomy and systematics of the pterosaur *Carniadactylus* (gen. n.) *rosenfeldi* (Dalla Vecchia, 1995)." *Rivista Italiana de Paleontologia e Stratigrafia* 115(2): 159–188.

18. Wild, R. (1978). "Die Flugsaurier (Reptilia, Pterosauria) aus der Oberen Trias von Cene bei Bergamo, Italien." *Bolletino della Societa Paleontologica Italiana* 17 (2): 176–256.

19. Buckland, W. (1835). "On the discovery of a new species of Pterodactyle in the Lias at Lyme Regis." *Transactions of the Geological Society of London*, series 23: 217–222.

20. Clark, J. M., J. A. Hopson, R. Hernandez, D. E. Fastovsky, and M. Montellano. (1998). "Foot posture in a primitive pterosaur." *Nature* 391: 886–889.

21. Sangster, S. (2001). "Anatomy, functional morphology and systematics of *Dimorphodon ,*" *Strata* 11: 87–88.

22. Wang, Xiaolin, Alexander W. A. Kellner, Shunxing Jiang, Xin Cheng, Xi Meng, and Taissa Rodriguez. (2010). "New long-tailed pterosaurs (Wukongopteridae) from western Liaoning, China." *Anais da Academia Brasileira de Ciências* 82 (4): 1045–1062.

23. Lü, J., D. M. Unwin, X. Jin, Y. Liu, and Q. Ji. (2010). "Evidence for modular evolution in a long-tailed pterosaur with a pterodactyloid skull." *Proceedings of the Royal Society B* 277(1680): 383–389.

24. Lü, J., L. Xu, H. Chang, and X. Zhang. (2011). "A new darwinopterid ptero-saur from the Middle Jurassic of western Liaoning, northeastern China and its ecological implications." *Acta Geologica Sinica - English Edition* 85(3): 507–514.

25. Lü, J., D. M. Unwin, D. C. Deeming, X. Jin, Y. Liu, and Q. Ji. (2011). "An egg-adult association, gender, and reproduction in pterosaurs." *Science* 331(6015): 321–324.

26. Rjabinin, A. N. (1948). "Remarks on a flying reptile from the Jurassic of the Kara-Tau." *Akademia Nauk, Paleontological Institute, Trudy* 15(1): 86–93.

27. Bennett, S. C. (2007). "A second specimen of the pterosaur *Anurognathus ammoni.*" *Paläontologische Zeitschrift* 81: 376–398.

28. Witton, M. P. (2008). "A new approach to determining pterosaur body mass and its implications for pterosaur flight." *Zitteliania* B28: 143–159.

29. Wang, X., Z. Zhou, F. Zhang, and X. Xu. (2002). "A nearly completely articulated rhamphorhynchoid pterosaur with exceptionally well-preserved wing membranes and 'hairs' from Inner Mongolia, northeast China." *Chinese Science Bulletin* 47(3): 226 – 232.

30. Dalla Vecchia, F. M. (2002). "Observations on the non-pterodactyloid pterosaur *Jeholopterus ningchengensis* from the Early Cretaceous of Northeastern China." *Natura Nascosta* 24: 8–27.

31. Peters, D. (2003). "The Chinese vampire and other overlooked pterosaur ptreasures." *Journal of Vertebrate Paleontology* 23(3): 87A.

32. Ji, S.-A., and Q. Ji. (1998). "A new fossil pterosaur (Rhamphorhynchoidea) from Liaoning." *Jiangsu Geology* 22(4):199–206.

33. Ji, S.-A., Q. Ji, and K. Padian. (1999). Biostratigraphy of new pterosaurs from China. *Nature* 398:573–574.

34. Unwin, D. M., J. Lü, and N. N. Bakhurina. (2000). "On the systematic and stratigraphic significance of pterosaurs from the Lower Cretaceous Yixian Formation (Jehol Group) of Liaoning, China." *Mitt. Mus. Naturk. Berlin Geowiss*. Reihe 3:181–206.

35. Lü, Junchang, and Xiaohui Fucha. (2010). "A new pterosaur (Pterosauria) from Middle Jurassic Tiaojishan Formation of western Liaoning, China." *Global Geology* 13 (3/4): 113–118.

36. Arbour, Victoria M., and Philip J. Currie. (2011). "An istiodactylid pterosaur from the Upper Cretaceous Nanaimo Group, Hornby Island, British Columbia, Canada." *Canadian Journal of Earth Sciences* 48 (1): 63–69.

37. Witton, M. P. (2012). "New Insights into the Skull of *Istiodactylus latidens* (Ornithocheiroidea, Pterodactyloidea)." *PLoS ONE* 7(3): e33170.

38. Wang, X., A. W. A. Kellner, Z. Zhou, and D. de Almeida Campos. (2005). "Pterosaur diversity and faunal turnover in Cretaceous terrestrial ecosystems in China." *Nature* 437:875–879.

39. Lü, Juchang, and Qiang Ji. (2006). "Preliminary results of a phylogenetic analysis of the pterosaurs from western Liaoning and surrounding area." *Journal of the Paleontological Society of Korea* 22(1):239–261.

40. Martill, D. M., and D. M. Unwin. (2011). "The world's largest toothed pterosaur, NHMUK R481, an incomplete rostrum of *Coloborhynchus capito* (Seeley 1870) from the Cambridge Greensand of England." *Cretaceous Research*, (advance online publication).

41. Rodrigues, T., and A. W. A. Kellner (2013). "Taxonomic review of the Ornithocheirus complex (Pterosauria) from the Cretaceous of England." *ZooKeys* 308: 1–112.

42. Andres, B., and T. S. Myers. (2013). "Lone Star Pterosaurs." *Earth and Environmental Science Transactions of the Royal Society of Edinburgh* 103: 1.

43. Sayão, J. M. , and A. W. A. Kellner. (2000). "Description of a pterosaur rostrum from the Crato Member, Santana Formation (Aptian-Albian) northeastern, Brazil." *Boletim do Museu Nacional* 54: 1–8.

44. Veldmeijer, A. J. (2003). "Description of *Coloborhynchus spielbergi* sp. nov. (Pterodactyloidea) from the Albian (Lower Cretaceous) of Brazil." *Scripta Geologica* 125: 35–139.

45. Veldmeijer, A. J. (2003). "Preliminary description of a skull and wing of a Brazilian lower Cretaceous (Santana Formation; Aptian-Albian) pterosaur (Pterodactyloidea) in the collection of the AMNH." *PalArch, series vertebrate palaeontology* 1–13.

46. Witton, M. P. (2012). "New Insights into the Skull of *Istiodactylus latidens* (Ornithocheiroidea, Pterodactyloidea)." *PLoS ONE* 7(3): e33170.

47. Andres, B., and Quiang Ji. (2006). "A new species of *Istiodactylus* (Pterosauria, Pterodactyloidea) from the Lower Cretaceous of Liaoning, China." *Journal of Vertebrate Paleontology* 26: 70–78.

48. Witmer, L. M., S. Chatterjee, J. Franzosa, and T. Rowe. (2003). "Neuroanatomy of flying reptiles and implications for flight, posture and behaviour." *Nature* 425(6961): 950–954.

49. Campos, D. A., and A. W. A. Kellner. (1985). "Panorama of the Flying Reptiles Study in Brazil and South America (Pterosauria/ Pterodactyloidea/ Anhangueridae)." *Anais da Academia Brasileira de Ciências* 57(4):141–142 & 453–466.

50. Wang, Xiaolin, and Junchang Lü. (2001). "Discovery of a pterodactloid pterosaur from the Yixian Formation of western Liaoning, China." *Chinese Science Bulletin* 45(12):447–454.

51. Vullo, R., and D. Neraudeau. (2009). "Pterosaur Remains from the Cenomanian (Late Cretaceous) Paralic Deposits of Charentes, Western France." *Journal of Vertebrate Paleontology* 29(1):277–282.

52. Fastnacht, M. (2001). "First record of Coloborhynchus (Pterosauria) from the Santana Formation (Lower Cretaceous) of the Chapada do Araripe of Brazil." *Paläontologisches Zeitschrift* 75: 23–36.

53. Hooley, R. W. (1914). "On the Ornithosaurian genus Ornithocheirus, with a Review of the Specimens from the Cambridge Greensand in the Sedgwick Museums, Cambridge." *Annals and Magazine of Natural History* 8 (78): 529–557.

54. Lee, Y.-N. (1994). "The Early Cretaceous Pterodactyloid Pterosaur Coloborhynchus from North America." *Palaeontology* 37 (4): 755–763.

55. Rodrigues, Taissa, and A. W. A. Kellner. (2009). "Review of the peterodactyloid pterosaur *Coloborhynchus*." *Zitteliana*, B28: 219–228.

56. Steel, L., D. M. Martill, D. M. Unwin, and J. D. Winch. (2005). "A new pterodactyloid pterosaur from the Wessex Formation (Lower Cretaceous) of the Isle of Wight, England." *Cretaceous Research* 26: 686–698.

57. Padian, K. (1983). "A functional analysis of flying and walking in pterosaurs." *Paleobiology* 9(3):218–239.

58. Kellner, A. W. A. (2010). "Comments on the Pteranodontidae (Pterosauria, Pterodactyloidea) with the description of two new species." *Anais da Academia Brasileira de Ciências* 82 (4): 1063–1084.

59. Lü, J. (2010). "A new boreopterid pterodactyloid pterosaur from the Early Cretaceous Yixian Formation of Liaoning Province, northeastern China." *Acta Geologica Sinica* 24: 241–246.

60. Bennett, S. C. (1996). "Year-classes of pterosaurs from the Solnhofen Limestone of Germany: Taxonomic and Systematic Implications." *Journal of Vertebrate Paleontology* 16(3): 432–444.

61. Jouve, S. (2004). "Description of the skull of a *Ctenochasma* (Pterosauria) from the latest Jurassic of eastern France, with a taxonomic revision of European Tithonian Pterodactyloidea." *Journal of Vertebrate Paleontology* 24(3): 542–554.

62. Bennett, S. C. (2007). "A review of the pterosaur *Ctenochasma*: taxonomy and ontogeny." *Neues Jahrbuch für Geologie und Paläontologie - Abhandlungen* 245(1): 23–31.

63. Martill, David M. (2011). "A new pterodactyloid pterosaur from the Santana Formation (Cretaceous) of Brazil." *Cretaceous Research* 32 (2): 236–243.

64. Jiang, Shunxing, and Xiaolin Wang. (2011). "A new ctenochasmatid pterosaur from the Lower Cretaceous, western Liaoning, China." *Anais da Academia Brasileira de Ciencias* 83 (4): 1243–1249.

65. Howse, S. C. B., and A. R. Milner. (1995). "The pterodactyloids from the Purbeck Limestone Formation of Dorset." *Bulletin of the Natural History Museum, London (Geology)* 51(1):73–88.

66. Leonardi, G., and G. Borgomanero. (1985). "*Cearadactylus atrox* nov. gen., nov. sp.: novo Pterosauria (Pterodactyloidea) da Chapada do Araripe, Ceara, Brasil." *Resumos dos communicaçoes VIII Congresso bras. de Paleontologia e Stratigrafia* 27: 75–80.

67. Vila Nova, Bruno C., A. W. A. Kellner, and Juliana M. Sayão, "Short Note on the Phylogenetic Position of *Cearadactylus Atrox*, and Comments Regarding Its Relationships to Other Pterosaurs", *Acta Geoscientica Sinica* 31 Supp.1: 73–75.

68. Unwin, D. M. (2002). "On the systematic relationships of Cearadactylus atrox, an enigmatic Early Cretaceous pterosaur from the Santana Formation of Brazil." *Mitteilungen Museum für Naturkunde Berlin, Geowissenschaftlichen Reihe* 5: 239–263.

69. Wang, X., A. W. A. Kellner, Z. Zhou, and D. A. Campos. (2007). "A new pterosaur (Ctenochasmatidae, Archaeopterodactyloidea) from the Lower Cretaceous Yixian Formation of China." *Cretaceous Research* 28(2): 2245–260.

70. Jiang, Shunxing, and Xiaolin Wang. (2011). "Important features of *Gegepterus changae* (Pterosauria: Archaeopterodactyloidea, Ctenochasmatidae) from a new specimen." *Vertebrata Palasiatica* 49(2): 172–184.

71. Andres, B., and Q. Ji. (2008). "A new pterosaur from the Liaoning Province of China, the phylogeny of the Pterodactyloidea, and convergence in their cervical vertebrae." *Palaeontology* 51 (2): 453–469.

72. Lü, J. (2009) "A baby pterodactyloid pterosaur from the Yixian Formation of Ningcheng, Inner Mongolia, China." *Acta Geologica Sinica* 83 (1): 1–8.

73. Schweigert, G. (2007). "Ammonite biostratigraphy as a tool for dating Upper Jurassic lithographic limestones from South Germany – first results and open questions." *Neues Jahrbuch für Geologie und Paläontologie – Abhandlungen* 245 (1): 117–125.

74. Bennett, S. C. (2013). "New information on body size and cranial display structures of *Pterodactylus antiquus*, with a revision of the genus." *Paläontologische Zeitschrift*.

75. Bennett, S. C. (2002). "Soft tissue preservation of the cranial crest of the pterosaur Germanodactylus from Solnhofen." *Journal of Vertebrate Paleontology* 22 (1): 43–48.

76. Lü, J., Y. Azuma, Z. Dong, R. Barsbold, Y. Kobayashi, and Y.-N. Lee. (2009). "New material of dsungaripterid pterosaurs (Pterosauria: Pterodactyloidea) from western Mongolia and its palaeoecological implications." *Geological Magazine* 146(5): 690–700.

77. Maisch, M. W., A. T. Matzke, and Ge Sun. (2004). "A new dsungaripteroid pterosaur from the Lower Cretaceous of the southern Junggar Basin, north-west China." *Cretaceous Research* 25:625–634.

78. Unwin, David M., and Wolf-Dieter Heinrich. (1999). "On a pterosaur jaw from the Upper Jurassic of Tendaguru (Tanzania)." *Mitteilungen aus dem Museum Für Naturkunde in Berlin Geowissenschaftliche Reihe* 2: 121–134.

79. Wang, X., A. W. A. Kellner, Z. Zhou, and D. A. Campos. (2008). "Discovery of a rare arboreal forest-dwelling flying reptile (Pterosauria, Pterodactyloidea) from China." *Proceedings of the National Academy of Sciences* 106(6): 1983–1987.

80. Martill, D. M., E. Frey, G. C. Diaz, and C. M. Bell. (2000). "Reinterpretation of a Chilean pterosaur and the occurrence of Dsungeripteridae in South America." *Geological Magazine* 137(1):19–25.

81. Casamiquela, R. M.(1975). "*Herbstosaurus pigmaeus* (Coeluria, Compsognathidae) n. gen. n. sp. del Jurásic medio del Neuquén (Patagonia septentrional). Uno de los más pequeños dinosaurios conocidos." *Actas del Primer Congreso Argentino de Paleontologia y Bioestratigrafia, Tucumán* 2: 87–103.

82. Galton, P. M. (1981). "A rhamphorhynchoid pterosaur from the Upper Jurassic of North America." *Journal of Paleontology* 55(5): 1117–1122.

83. Zhongjian, Yang. (1964). "On a new pterosaurian from Sinkiang, China." *Vertebrata PalAsiatic* 8: 221–255.

84. Buffetaut, E., J.-J. Lepage, and G. Lepage. (1998). "A new pterodactyloid pterosaur from the Kimmeridgian of the Cap de la Hève (Normandy, France)." *Geological Magazine* 135(5):719–722.

85. Witton, M. P., D. M. Martill, and R. F. Loveridge. (2010). "Clipping the Wings of Giant Pterosaurs: Comments on Wingspan Estimations and Diversity." *Acta Geoscientica Sinica* 31 Supp.1: 79–81.

86. Witton, M. P., and M. B. Habib. (2010). "On the Size and Flight Diversity of Giant Pterosaurs, the Use of Birds as Pterosaur Analogues and Comments on Pterosaur Flightlessness." *PLoS ONE* 5(11): e13982.

87. Lü, J., and B. K. Zhang. (2005). "New pterodactyloid pterosaur from the Yixian Formation of western Liaoning." *Geological Review* 51 (4): 458–462.

88. Nessov, L. A. (1984). "Upper Cretaceous pterosaurs and birds from Central Asia." *Paleontologicheskii Zhurnal* 1984(1): 47–57.

89. Humphries, S., R. H. C. Bonser, M. P. Witton, and D. M. Martill. (2007). "Did pterosaurs feed by skimming? Physical modelling and anatomical evaluation of an unusual feeding method." *PLoS Biology* 5(8): e204.

90. Lü, J., D. M. Unwin, L. Xu, and X. Zhang. (2008). "A new azhdarchoid pterosaur from the Lower Cretaceous of China and its implications for pterosaur phylogeny and evolution." *Naturwissenschaften.*

91. Kellner, A. W. A., and D. A. Campos. (2007). "Short note on the ingroup relationships of the Tapejaridae (Pterosauria, Pterodactyloidea)." *Boletim do Museu Nacional* 75: 1–14.

92. Kellner, A. W. A., and D. A. Campos. (1988). "Sobre un novo pterossauro com crista sagital da Bacia do Araripe, Cretaceo Inferior do Nordeste do Brasil. (Pterosauria, Tupuxuara, Cretaceo, Brasil)." *Anais de Academia Brasileira de Ciências* 60: 459–469.

93. Kellner, A. W. A., and D. A. Campos. (1994). "A new species of *Tupuxuara* (Pterosauria, Tapejaridae) from the Early Cretaceous of Brazil." *An. Acad. brasil. Ciênc.* 66: 467–473.

94. Witton, M. P. (2009). "A new species of *Tupuxuara* (Thalassodromidae, Azhdarchoidea) from the Lower Cretaceous Santana Formation of Brazil, with a note on the nomenclature of Thalassodromidae." *Cretaceous Research* 30(5): 1293–1300.

95. Averianov, A. O. (2007). "New records of azhdarchids (Pterosauria, Azhdarchidae) from the late Cretaceous of Russia, Kazakhstan, and Central Asia." *Paleontological Journal* 41 (2): 189–197.

96. Witton, M. P., and D. Naish. (2008). "A Reappraisal of Azhdarchid Pterosaur Functional Morphology and Paleoecology." *PLoS ONE* 3(5): e2271.

97. Lawson, D. A. (1975). "Pterosaur from the Latest Cretaceous of West Texas. Discovery of the Largest Flying Creature." *Science* 187: 947–948.

98. Kellner, A. W. A., and W. Langston. (1996). "Cranial remains of *Quetzalcoatlus* (Pterosauria, Azhdarchidae) from Late Cretaceous sediments of Big Bend National Park, Texas." *Journal of Vertebrate Paleontology* 16: 222–231.

99. Henderson, M. D., and J. E. Peterson. (2006). "An azhdarchid pterosaur cervical vertebra from the Hell Creek Formation (Maastrichtian) of southeastern Montana." *Journal of Vertebrate Paleontology* 26(1): 192–195.

100. Currie, Philip J., and Aase Roland Jacobsen. (1995). "An azhdarchid pterosaur eaten by a velociraptorine theropod." *Canadian Journal of Earth Science* 32: 922–925.

ZHAO Chuang and YANG Yang
&
PNSO's Scientific Art Projects Plan: Stories on Earth (2010–2070)

ZHAO Chuang and YANG Yang are two professionals who work together to create scientific art. Mr. ZHAO Chuang, a scientific artist, and Ms. YANG Yang, an author of scientific children's books, started working together when they jointly founded PNSO, an organization devoted to the research and creation of scientific art in Beijing on June 1, 2010. A few months later, they launched Scientific Art Projects Plan: Stories on Earth (2010–2070). The plan uses scientific art to create a captivating, historically accurate narrative. These narratives are based on the latest scientific research, focusing on the complex relationships between species, natural environments, communities, and cultures. The narratives consider the perspectives of human civilizations while exploring Earth's past, present, and future. The PNSO founders plan to spend 60 years to do research and create unique and engaging scientific art and literature for people around the world. They hope to share scientific knowledge through publications, exhibitions, and courses. PNSO's overarching goal is to serve research institutions and the general public, especially young people.

PNSO has independently completed or participated in numerous creative and research projects. The organization's work has been shared with and loved by thousands of people around the world. PNSO collaborates with professional scientists and has been invited to many key laboratories around the world to create scientific works of art. Many works produced by PNSO staff members have been published in leading journals, including *Nature*, *Science*, and *Cell*. The organization has always been committed to supporting state-of-the-art scientific explorations. In addition, a large number of illustrations completed by PNSO staff members have been published and cited in hundreds of well-known media outlets, including the *New York Times*, the *Washington Post*, the *Guardian*, *Asahi Shimbun*, the *People's Daily*, BBC, CNN, Fox News, and CCTV. The works created by PNSO staff members have been used to help the public better understand the latest scientific discoveries and developments. In the public education sector, PNSO has held joint exhibitions with scientific organizations including the American Museum of Natural History and the Chinese Academy of Sciences. PNSO has also completed international cooperation projects with the World Young Earth Scientist Congress and the Earth Science Matters Foundation, thus helping young people in different parts of the world understand and appreciate scientific art.

KEY PROJECTS

I. Darwin: An Art Project of Life Sciences

*The models are all life-sized and are based on fossils found around the world

1.1 Dinosaur fossils

1.2 Pterosaurs fossils

1.3 Aquatic reptile fossils

1.4 Ancient mammals of the Cenozoic Era

1.5 Chengjiang biota: animals in the Early Cambrian from fossils discovered in Chengjiang, Yunnan, China

1.6 Jehol biota: animals in the Mesozoic Era from fossils discovered in Jehol, Western Liaoning, China

1.7 Early and extinct humans

1.8 Ancient animals that coexisted with early and extinct humans

1.9 Modern humans

1.10 Animals of the *Felidae* family

1.11 Animals of the *Canidae* family

1.12 Animals of the Proboscidea order